# EMOTION FULL

# EMOTION FULL

A Guide to Self-Care
for Your Mental Health
and Emotions

LAUREN WOODS

mango
PUBLISHING GROUP ™

CORAL GABLES

For permission requests, please contact the publisher at:
Mango Publishing Group
2850 Douglas Road, 2nd Floor
Coral Gables, FL 33134 USA
info@mango.bz

For special orders, quantity sales, course adoptions and corporate sales, please email the publisher at sales@mango.bz. For trade and wholesale sales, please contact Ingram Publisher Services at customer.service@ingramcontent.com or +1.800.509.4887.

**Emotionfull: A Guide to Self-Care for Your Mental Health and Emotions**
ISBNs: (p) 978-1-64250-356-2 (e) 978-1-64250-357-9
BISAC: SEL004000—SELF-HELP / Affirmations
LCCN: 2020940928

Printed in the United States of America

Please note some names have been changed to protect the privacy of individuals.

**This book is not intended as a substitute for the medical advice of physicians. The reader should consult a physician in matters relating to their mental and bodily health. Any suggestions contained herein adopted by the reader is done at their own risk. The author and publisher advise readers to take full responsibility for their safety and know their limits.**

# Table of Contents

## INTRODUCTION

# A Note from Lauren

Hello! I'm Lauren, the creator of The Positive Page, an online mental health support community. I wrote this book because I wanted to create something that could come in handy on days when you're full of difficult emotions. You may have picked up this book because you're struggling with your mental health right now, or maybe because you've struggled with it long-term—either way, it's totally valid for you to want help with that! I hope you find this book comforting in times when things feel a little bit intense.

You don't have to read it in order. In fact, not all of the sections will be relevant to how you're feeling, but you can skip to the parts that stand out to you. I hope you find at least one section that resonates with you in a comforting way and provides you with a sense of being understood. Take your time reading and highlight the parts you find helpful, so that you can easily find your favorite quotes or pieces of advice whenever you need them! Fold the pages, or even tear pages out. Use this book in whatever way will help you.

To me, being emotionfull means that your mind is filled with so many emotions that you feel overwhelmed. These emotions can be positive or negative, and having so many at the same time might mean you need a little help knowing what to do with them. Your feelings are such a powerful part of your everyday life, and if you're emotionfull, you should take some time to make sure you're prioritizing your mental health.

Before you start reading, I wanted to tell you a little bit about myself and why I wanted to make this book for you. I've been diagnosed with OCD (obsessive compulsive disorder) and health anxiety (hypochondria). I'm now twenty, but I've struggled with my mental health from a much younger age. It wasn't until I was fourteen that I realized what was happening to me and was able to tell someone. That realization came after years of feeling anxious and not knowing why, and losing sleep because of OCD-related fears and behaviors. I experienced years of struggling to eat, feeling upset, scared, and confused. I feared reaching out because I didn't know what an anxiety disorder was, let alone OCD. Years went by where I lived without proper support and didn't even know how to support myself. All of this was because of the lack of education and awareness around mental health. Had I known that my thoughts were not normal and causing my unhealthy behaviors, I would have done something sooner.

Things changed when I first reached out to my friends, one of which helped me tell my mom that I had been experiencing panic attacks. Opening up to my mom was terrifying. After that, it took another two years to find the right therapy to treat my illnesses, simply because of the lack of available space in mental health services. I did two years of irregular and short-term counseling, and even though it made me feel less alone, it wasn't what I needed to treat my disorders—even the counselors knew that. It took a long time to get help, but I finally got into child and adolescent mental health services (CAMHS) and started cognitive behavioral therapy (CBT), and am now under adult mental health services (AMHS), where I receive long-term treatment.

This is not a unique story—many people who I've had the opportunity to connect with through The Positive Page have dealt with mental illness from a young age without proper treatment too. Talking about my mental health was initially really difficult, even terrifying. But a few years after reaching out to my mom and getting support, I realized that I wanted to raise awareness and reach out to those who were also struggling. Talking about my mental health in this way—in an effort to raise awareness online—was just as scary. The first thing I had to process was the fact that I was allowed to talk about my mental health without feeling guilty or stupid. I struggled with that thought because, even though I talked about how "difficult" my life was, I recognized I am also very lucky. For starters, I am white and live in a safe neighborhood in the UK—those are privileges in and of themselves. I have also grown up in a loving family that is financially stable. These factors make me more fortunate than many other people in the world. You might be feeling this guilt as well. If you are, I want you to know that I understand how you feel.

Eventually, I realized that I couldn't spend my whole life feeling guilty and dismissing my anxious feelings simply because of the fortunate circumstances of my life/upbringing. Something that helped change my perspective was understanding the fact that mental illness doesn't care about the circumstances of your life. Anyone can be mentally ill. You may have things in your life that should make you happy and mentally well, but a mental illness can still affect you regardless of the presence of those things. My mind doesn't work as well as it should—my thoughts are disordered, and that makes me react in ways I shouldn't, and think and feel things that distress and terrify me. OCD is a complex mental disorder, and I needed to validate that fact to not feel like I was being whiny or ungrateful in talking about how I felt. I realized that talking about it was good. Talking about it didn't make me self-centered or spoiled; it was my way of seeking treatment for my illness. This eventually led to my helping others feel like they could do the same.

Being mentally ill has affected every single part of my life—my education; my work; my physical health, eating habits, and weight; my social life, friends, family, and relationships; even my self-image and ability to do everyday things. Mental illness can knock you down until you're stuck in a cycle of unhealthy behaviors and constant mental torment. You can feel so exhausted that you don't know how or where to start trying to help yourself. I once described OCD as having a bully inside your brain, telling lies to make you feel like a bad person and making you too scared to do things. The most reassuring thing I've experienced on this journey was finding out that my thoughts had an explanation.

When I was fourteen, I went online to try and understand what was happening inside my head and found information about OCD. If you are struggling and feel like there may be something happening with your mental health, it's important to read up and talk to a doctor. You deserve the help, so don't ignore your feelings!

I felt like I was going insane, with my mind cultivating this never-ending stream of intrusive thoughts that made me feel guilty, scared, and bad about myself. It felt like everything was a challenge, everything could go wrong, everything would harm me. And it goes without saying that I hated it—I still do. I hated having a mental illness, I hated that it caused problems with everything I did and made everything feel so much more difficult. I hated having panic attacks at the most inconvenient times, and feeling like they inconvenienced the people I was with. I hated that the thoughts were always there, and that I felt like they would always be there. I hated how it affected my family. There were so many days that I sat crying, desperately saying, "I just want to be normal." I begged for the thoughts to go away, for me to not have to constantly feel such high levels of anxiety.

I am very glad to say that, as of writing this, I'm not there anymore. I've come far enough to not feel such huge volumes of anxiety every day, and my thoughts are calmer because I've learned better ways to manage them.

If you struggle with your mental health too, I hope you know are not alone. Fighting the intense feelings that come with poor mental health is not easy. Doing some mindfulness exercises, or using essential oils, or "just breathing," like many suggest, is not going to fix your disorder like magic. I know and recognize your struggle, even if our situations or diagnoses don't match up. I understand the absolute frustration that you feel trying to recover from a mental illness. I want you to know that it is possible for things to get easier, little by little, and with loads of bumps and dips in the road. Maybe you'll recover and stay that way for a long time; maybe, like me, you'll have to work on it every week to maintain as much stability as you can. It is possible.

If you have no idea where to start with recovery, if you're right in the middle of recovery, or even if you've recovered and are just having a bad day, I want you to have something to read when you feel stuck. Even if you don't have a mental illness at all, and just feel overwhelmed sometimes, I want you to feel supported and understood. I want you to know that there is hope, that you can find support and ways to manage being emotionfull. If you struggle with being overwhelmed, I want you to know that your feelings are valid and that you are not alone.

That being said, I feel that education is just as important. It is vital to teach people about the signs and symptoms of stress and mental health disorders, as well as how to *healthily* support those going through it. In response to the lack of accessible support, I decided in 2017 to begin building an online mental health awareness website.

Growing up with poor mental health and struggling to find professional support—and seeing this also happen to people I cared about—really affected me. I felt endlessly frustrated. That's why I built The Positive Page, a mental health community I run online. Making something online meant that anyone with the internet could access it, and while I know it's not equivalent to getting professional support, I wanted to do everything I could to help others that felt this way.

That's also why I've created this book: to share what I've learned in and out of therapy so far, how I currently deal with my mental health, and what things I think could help you. I am not a professional, just someone who has gone through it (and is still going through it!). Emotional self-care is vital to your mental health, so I hope that you take your mental well-being seriously and look after it as much as you can.

I want this book to be as easy to read as it can be. I know that, when you're struggling with your feelings, you're probably not going to want to sit and read pages and pages of writing. For example, if you're having a panic attack, you want help as fast as possible and are likely to find it hard to concentrate. That's why I wrote this in such a way that you can skip to the parts you want to read, when you need to read them. The chapters are short and to the point, that way you don't have to read everything all at once. However, if you're not in need of immediate help, you can read it consecutively if you want—you may find help in unexpected places!

# PART 1

# TELLING SOMEONE

## CHAPTER 1

# When You're Struggling to Reach Out

Reaching out is hard, but please know this: it's okay for you to tell someone how you feel. A lot of people feel that reaching out is like seeking attention, but it's not—at least not in the way that you think. If you're struggling, getting someone's attention can provide the support and help that you deserve. Often, we feel our struggles are insignificant when compared to the struggles of others. But the thing is, no matter what anyone else is experiencing, you also deserve the best chance at living a happy life. Everyone deserves that. If there's something that affects your happiness, then you need to seek whatever help there is to make it easier for you.

I often hear from people who feel like they have to suffer on their own because they think their issues aren't "big" enough to justify asking for help. If you've felt like this and it's kept you from telling someone, you may be struggling with your self-esteem. The problem isn't that your struggles aren't big enough, it's that you've never given them the validation they deserve. Your mind is probably saying, "It's nothing, and people don't need to listen to my problems." By thinking this, you're not giving yourself importance. When you validate your needs, your mind would instead say something like, "I'm finding things really hard, and that matters." This could then help you believe you deserve support for your feelings. There is no set criteria that dictates who is and isn't allowed to ask for help. Your problem is not "too small." If you're struggling with your mental health in any way, it affects your life, and that's worth paying attention to.

If you are struggling to validate your feelings, remember a few things:

- No matter how "small" your issue is, you're still allowed to ask for help.

- You don't have to be at your worst to ask for help.

- You don't have to be "struggling more" than anyone else to ask for help. There's no shame in it. Even if your problem *is* "small," it would be so much better for you to ask for help early on than stay silent and potentially let it get worse.

## STARTING THE CONVERSATION

You might be thinking, "How on earth do I tell someone I'm struggling with my mental health? How do I even start?" You're not alone! In fact, most people wonder these same things, especially the first time. There are a couple of routes you can take to start a conversation about your mental health.

1.  **Have a heart-to-heart with someone you care about.**

    Sit down with a person you're close to and talk to them. This may seem obvious, but for a lot of people this can be the hardest thing. Find a spark of courage inside yourself, take the leap, and say the words you need. To make this easier, I suggest first preparing what you would like to say in your head. You could even make a bullet point list, or note down some sentence starters. Go into the conversation with the first sentence mapped out. The first sentence is usually the hardest, but once you have their attention and know what you want to say, that breaks down the initial wall. The person you're talking to is part of the conversation, too, so the pressure isn't all on you. They will ask questions and make conversation with you.

The first sentence will vary depending on what it is you're finding hard and how much you want to tell them, but here are a few examples:

- "Can we talk? I am really struggling and don't know how to deal with it on my own."
- "I'm finding it difficult to do...(X,Y, Z)."
- "For a little while, I have been feeling very _____, and I find it difficult to talk about. Some advice or support would be really helpful."
- "I'm struggling a lot with my mental health and think I need professional support."
- "I don't know what's happening, but my feelings are very scary at the moment. Can you please help me?"
- "Things have been feeling a little overwhelming recently..."

These sentences may feel daunting, but they can open conversations that could really benefit you.

2. **Go straight to a professional or doctor.**

   If talking to someone close to you is too difficult right now, but you still want help, you can go to someone you're not familiar with. Most people go to their doctor, tell them they've been finding it hard to cope with their mental health, and ask for professional support. You can also self-refer to a mental health facility, like counseling, therapy, or an inpatient ward. Depending on what country you're in, availability for each of these is different; it's worth doing some online research to see what is available in your area. Other people have also reached out to school guidance counselors, youth workers, and teachers for support and advice. For some people, the thought of talking to a stranger is less daunting than talking to someone they're close to. I find this true for myself, and though it's taken me a long time to work out why that is, I've come to this conclusion: the reactions of people I don't know don't matter to me as much, because there's no connection at risk. Their opinions of me don't matter as much as those of the people I love.

3.  Write a letter (or send a text) to someone you know that expresses everything you're finding hard.

    Saying the words out loud is a challenge I've not yet battled. I still find talking to be socially overwhelming. When someone is waiting for you to say something, it can be difficult to find the courage to spit the words out. Writing down how I feel on paper or on my phone has been a godsend, and it can help you, too. You can write a text or a letter with exactly what you want to say, and then all you have to do is find the courage to press send or hand the paper over. You can make these messages as long or as short as you want. They can simply state that you're struggling and you need help, or describe at length how you are/have been feeling. If you're finding it hard to explain how you feel, try breaking it down into two points: how you've been feeling, and in what way it's been making your life harder.

4.  Find a video or blog post that explains how you feel and send it to a friend.

    If writing how you feel is entirely out of the question because no words come to mind, it's okay to rely on the words of others to get the conversation started. Use the resources people have put out there for you. Search through YouTube for videos that explain your struggle. These videos can be from a medical perspective, or from someone telling their personal experience. Read through some blog posts from mental health bloggers and advocates, find a post that describes what you're going through, and send it to the person you want to tell. If you prefer, you can sit and watch or read with them face-to-face. On my website (www.thepositivepage.org), we share some mental health stories that may resonate with you. Another site that could help with this is The Mighty (www.themighty.com). There, you can find thousands of personal testimonies sharing people's journeys with their physical and mental health. I used The Mighty to read others' experiences with OCD and found a video called "I Have OCD. This Is What It's Like to Be in My Mind for 3 Minutes." This made me feel overwhelmingly understood. What I found so difficult to explain, this video described in such a personal way. I showed this video to my therapist, my mom, my aunt, and a couple of friends. I feel it really helped communicate how I was and am living with mental illness.

## WORRY BOXES

Throughout the seven parts of this book, there are chapters with what I call "Worry Boxes." On my website and Instagram, I run a submission box where anyone can anonymously send a paragraph or so about what they are struggling with. I do my best to answer those "Worry Box" submissions with advice, and decided to incorporate some of them into this book. It can be comforting to see that other people are experiencing similar worries—and some friendly advice is great, too.

## WORRY BOX: STIGMA AFFECTING YOUR SUPPORT SYSTEM

"I have been feeling quite bad the last couple months. Every time I try to explain this to my parents, they don't really listen. They say I'm overreacting, faking my problems, and harming myself for attention. Even others have tried to tell them, but they just don't see it. I'm so desperate..."

Not having the support of your parents must be really hard. I want you to know that you're not alone and that your feelings are important. You don't deserve to be ignored. Feeling low and self-harming is not "overreacting" or "attention-seeking"—this is a negative coping mechanism that deserves attention and support. Lack of support often comes from misunderstanding; helping your parents understand what you're going through is the best way to help the three of you communicate. Find some informational posts, videos, and websites to send to your parents with helpful explanations of what self-harm is and what causes it.

Even though I understand why it can be helpful, you don't need your parents' permission to reach out to organizations and mental health professionals. I don't know where you are in the world, but it's worth investigating what support is available in your area and seeing where you can go. Alternatively, you can make an appointment with a doctor and explain to them how you've been feeling. If getting help is something that's not possible at the moment, then I suggest trying to find some healthy coping mechanisms you can do yourself. Find a distraction for when you're feeling the urge to self-harm. This can be any activity you like, so long as it isn't dangerous to your health.

I completely understand that this may all seem daunting, but it's really important that you take your feelings seriously.

CHAPTER 2

# When You're Confused about Your Mental Health

Emotions are confusing. I totally get it. Part of the difficulty of dealing with poor mental health is the inability to understand what's happening inside your mind. Once you define that, however, it's easier to talk about, treat, and process it. Understanding yourself is a very personal thing—only you can tell how you're feeling and what you're finding difficult. In case you didn't know, here are some basics on mental health that might help you out.

Everyone has a state of "mental health." According to Mentalhealth.gov, the term "mental health" encompasses your emotional, psychological, and social well-being—all of which comprise the state of your *mental* well-being. Think of it in the same way as physical health: everyone has a body and a state of physical health, therefore everyone also has a brain and a state of mental health. The difference is that some people's mental states are healthy, and some people's are not. When someone is "mentally ill," it means that their mental health is disordered. More often than not, people don't understand the difference between the two terms. I always hear people say, "I don't have mental health," when what they actually mean to say is, "I don't have a mental illness." Although it may seem petty to make a clear distinction between these two words, it's really important.

When someone refers to "mental health" as something that's alien to them, as if it's something they can't or don't "have," it reinforces the idea that it's something people can't understand. However, the most important thing to know is that everyone has a state of mental health, and thus anyone can experience a mental illness at any point in their lifetime. The more we cast away the term "mental health" into a box of confusion, the more we are at risk of struggling (or seeing someone else struggle) and not catching the signs.

We need to understand that someone can be struggling with their mental health without having a mental illness. For example, you can get upset, have a bad week, or feel stressed or anxious for any number of reasons. Just because you feel this way for a few days doesn't mean you have a mental illness/disorder. (However, these are still valid feelings and you deserve support from your friends and family!). Think of it like a cold: it shows that you're struggling with your physical health, but it will go away in about a week or two. It doesn't necessarily mean you've got a long-term physical illness/disorder. Mental health works in the same way. Generally, to know if you're experiencing any type of long term-physical illness/disorder, you'd measure the length of time you've been experiencing symptoms. The same goes for mental health.

## LOOKING FOR THE SYMPTOMS OF MENTAL DISORDERS

If you want to work out whether or not you're struggling with a mental illness, the key is to educate yourself on the symptoms. Different mental disorders have different symptoms, and breaking down your mental state into symptoms can be difficult if you're confused about your mental health. However, there are a few general signs you can keep an eye out for:

- Look at the symptoms you can *see*, as opposed to your internal feelings, which can be harder to detect. Write a list of the things that have become *increasingly difficult* since you started having problems. A few areas to pay attention to can be: social habits (going out to school, meeting friends), eating habits, sleeping habits, physical self-care (exercising too much or too little, showering, or changing clothes), and the state of your relationships (seeing friends and family, wanting to meet new people).

⊙ From there, you can work out *why* those things are harder now. Spoiler alert: The reason is your feelings. List how you feel— anxious, depressed, sad, stressed, etc. Link that feeling to the behavior that has become increasingly difficult for you. For example, if you're finding it difficult to meet friends, what feelings are you experiencing when trying to do this?

⊙ Then comes the hardest part: listing the thoughts you're experiencing. For example, when you try to meet a friend and you feel anxious, what are the thoughts you have just before or while trying to do this? If you cannot understand your thoughts right now, that's okay; you can work out enough from your behavior and feelings to know that you're struggling.

⊙ The final step is reflecting on what you've discovered. How often are these thoughts and feelings affecting your life? Do you know where they originated from or what caused them? Do you know how to handle them yourself, or do you need extra support? It's okay not to know these answers; this is when it's helpful to talk to a doctor.

This exercise is only a starting point to help those who are worried about reaching out. Please do not take this as a guide to diagnose yourself. Contact a professional for this!

Taking this step by step might help you understand a tiny bit more about what thoughts and feelings in your mind are making life feel harder. It can also help undo some confusion you may have on the huge topic of mental health. After you've worked out some of your struggles, the next step would be to contact a professional to help reach a diagnosis, should you need one. If you don't, the professional can at least talk things over with you to help you out of the rough period you're in.

## SIGNS YOUR MENTAL HEALTH MAY BE SUFFERING

Simply taking the first step toward acknowledging your struggle is the hardest part. If you're experiencing any one of the signs listed below,

know that you're not alone. It's okay to have these
symptoms when you're going through something.

- Finding it difficult to concentrate
  on anything.
- Spending a lot of time consumed by
  your thoughts.
- Feeling unable to think straight.
- Feeling generally stressed or overwhelmed.
- Feeling easily irritable/defensive.
- Struggling to sleep.
- Struggling to eat.
- Distancing yourself from people or not
  wanting to spend time with people.
- Feeling physically or mentally tired all of the
  time (your mental health can have a big effect
  on your energy levels).
- Feeling overwhelmed by everyday
  things (getting dressed, brushing teeth,
  preparing food).
- Forgetting things.
- Feeling like you're floating.
- Spending a large amount of time just staring
  at things/zoning out.
- Crying more than usual.

CHAPTER 3

# Getting to Know Your Triggers

You may have heard the word "trigger" used before. I certainly have, and not in a good way. When I was in high school, the word "trigger" was thrown around as a joke. If someone was the slightest bit annoyed at something, kids would say, for example, "Ben's been triggered," and laugh about it. Even though it seems harmless, this used to get under my skin. I was dealing with sometimes debilitating triggers, which at the time were very confusing for me, and people were going around making jokes about those feelings. This made me feel as if I couldn't talk about being triggered in a serious way.

In mental health, a trigger is something that causes a pattern of thoughts, feelings, and behaviors to happen, often provoking a distressed response. If you have a mental disorder, you're probably already aware of a lot of your own triggers. If you see a therapist, you've definitely worked on discussing these together. As not everyone has access to this service, I wanted to write about identifying triggers to assist those who do not. For me, learning to identify my triggers helped a lot, and I want to help others do the same.

Identifying triggers can be easier in some cases than in others. Think back to the last time you were feeling anxious or low. What happened before you started feeling this way?

Once I started to identify my triggers, I was able to understand how and why I felt the way I did. It makes sense, doesn't it? How can you battle something when you don't know what it is? I learned that I had some triggers that happened regularly, and some that came out of very specific situations. However, my responses to all of my triggers were disordered and unhealthy. Now that I'm aware of that, it's easier to see both the things that make my anxiety worse and the things that stop feeding it. If you want to read more about the cycle of feeding triggers, go to part 6 of this book.

## IDENTIFYING TRIGGERS

Fill in this chart when you're experiencing difficult feelings and behaviors and you're not sure why. We can sometimes be triggered without realizing why.

### HOW ARE YOU FEELING?

_____
_____

### WRITE DOWN WHAT YOU'VE DONE TODAY:

_____
_____
_____
_____
_____

### WHAT THOUGHTS ARE YOU EXPERIENCING?

_____
_____
_____
_____

---

### HOW ARE YOU FEELING?

_____
_____

### WRITE DOWN WHAT YOU'VE DONE TODAY:

_____
_____
_____
_____
_____

### WHAT THOUGHTS ARE YOU EXPERIENCING?

_____
_____
_____
_____

## WORRY BOX: TALKING TO YOUR FAMILY

"I've been diagnosed with PTSD, MDD, Generalized Anxiety Disorder and Anorexia, but I'm nineteen and therefore none of my family know. I'm not sure if or how I should tell them. I'm currently on medication and on a waiting list to start therapy (I've been waiting over seven months) and don't know how they'll react (even though our family has a history of depression). Any advice on what to do?"

It is 100 percent your decision to whom you open up about your mental health and when you're ready to do so. There is no pressure to tell anyone right away. However, if you feel ready and want someone's support, then it's okay to reach out and tell them. I completely understand that this can be really hard to do, and saying the words out loud might be really scary. If you can't find the words, there are other ways you can tell them. You could try writing it down or sending a long message (even if you're sitting next to them). Check out the "Starting the Conversation" section in chapter 1 for more ideas. You could also emotionally prepare if you're worried that they will react negatively, though I really, really hope they don't. If they do, know that you don't deserve that. Your feelings are important and valid no matter what. You could give them a little list of things they could do to help, or a list of things that wouldn't help so they know not to do those. If you choose to tell someone, I wish you good luck!

## WORRY BOX: TALKING TO A THERAPIST

"I'm currently trying to seek help for trauma-related issues and anxiety. But the issue I'm having most trouble with is reaching out to therapists in the first place. It is giving me anxiety just knowing that I have to take that initial step. Also, I'm worried that we may not be a good fit or they'll try and hurt me (trauma-related) and I won't be able to stop them. I know that I want help and need it more than anything so that I can get to the person I've always dreamed I would become, but I'd love advice on how to get through this short phase of apprehension."

This is a really tough situation, and I'm really sorry you're struggling with going to therapy. I don't know the right or wrong way to go about it, but my advice would be to take things one step at a time. First, reach out to a doctor, talk to them about how you're feeling and what you're struggling with. They will then refer you to a mental health professional. The second step would be to just go to the initial appointment where they typically just assess you. Next, go to the first therapy appointment and see if you think you'd get along with the therapist. If not, you're allowed to ask about seeing a different person. The process of finding the right therapist could take months, but it's okay to take things slowly. This can clearly be really scary, but breaking it down might make it more manageable. You can stop the process at any time, too.

## WORRY BOX: RECOVERY

> "I am worried I will never recover from my mental illness and be stuck the rest of my life."

My advice for the person who submitted this is, firstly, that you're not alone in this feeling. Recovery is hard—really, really hard—but it is possible. No matter how many setbacks you have, you can ultimately have an easier and more fulfilling life. It takes a lot of work to engage in therapy and face scary things, but you can get better. Not everyone feels that they recover from mental illness to the point that it's completely gone. However, millions of people recover to the point where they can function and enjoy life, where they can reach their dreams and goals. It is possible and YOU can do it, too. I would suggest reading some stories of people who have overcome their mental illnesses; this can help prove the possibility that it doesn't have to be like this forever.

## PART 2

# YOU'RE BIGGER THAN WHAT'S MAKING YOU ANXIOUS

## CHAPTER 4

# Battling Anxieties

Something that might help you battle your anxiety is finding the right voice with which to talk to yourself. Everyone does this differently, and it's okay to test it out and try finding a way that makes you feel better. The first step I took to find my voice was to work out how I wanted to see my disorder. Often, these voices start with either "I," "You," or "We."

First, say to yourself the phrases:

- "You can do this."
- "'I can do this."
- "We can do this."

Which one feels better to you? Are you unsure? Here's how I how I found my voice.

Most of the time, before you get help for anxiety, you think of it as part of your identity. You're probably thinking, "Of course, my emotions are a part of me," and that is true, they are. However, I've found it helpful to think of my anxiety disorders as things that are *other* than me, external things that make my life a little difficult. I do this so much that now, I never talk about my anxiety disorders as part of myself, but always as external things that are affecting me.

For example, I say: "My anxiety thinks..."

Rather than: "I think..."

I like to think of it is as different versions of me. There's the Lauren who is fully capable of doing scary things—that's the Lauren without a mental illness. Then there's the Lauren with OCD and anxiety who sees those things as terrifying and doesn't think she can do them. Healthy Lauren talks to unhealthy Lauren to help her do scary things. Of course, I know that there's only one of me, and that technically I don't have two brains, but it's a lot easier for me to talk to my anxiety in this way. As I view the two different versions of myself, the voice I use to speak to my anxiety is "We." I'm telling both sides of myself that they can *both* do scary things. The part of me that has a disorder can do it just as much as the part of me that does not.

Lots of people do this in different ways. Some people like to talk to themselves in first person because it gives them more confidence and empowerment to say "I can." Others like to externalize their mental disorders as an entirely different character and talk to them using second person ("You can"). This is a technique that some therapists use to help people understand their anxiety.

Here are some examples of how people do this:

1.  **Give it a name.**

    Personify your disorder, visualize it as another person/being. I once spoke to someone who called their anxiety "Alice" and visualized it as someone who needed help. This allowed her to be kind, patient, and compassionate toward herself, and stopped her from getting annoyed at herself for feeling anxious. Some people like to give their personified disorder a personality and not just a name.

2.  **Draw it.**

    Similarly to naming, I've seen people draw their mental disorder as another way of personifying it. They give it a color, size, and shape.

Personifying your mental illness can help you talk to it, and can therefore help you process your feelings. With anxiety, it's easy to respond to yourself with anger and frustration. But talking to it in whichever way feels best for you is a more effective way of supporting yourself.

If you regularly battle anxiety, it may be helpful to define the tipping point of when your anxiety turns into a panic attack. It's possible to feel anxious without having a panic attack, it just takes a lot of practice. Finding the point when you "lose control" of your feelings is the first step. Once you can tell when your anxiety levels reach that point, you need to put a healthy coping mechanism into practice. These help you stop doing the negative behaviors that anxiety encourages unnecessarily. Hopefully, these will also help decrease your chances of having a panic attack. This is something I have learned from a therapist, and even though it may not work every time, that's okay. Don't beat yourself up if you can't find the strength to battle anxiety. It's scary and hard, and that's *okay*. You can try again.

To me, fighting anxiety is like this: either anxiety is going to squash me or I am going to squash it! Sometimes I can't cope with my overwhelming feelings and have a panic attack, but sometimes I manage to talk to myself with enough affirmations to tackle the panic. Once my anxiety gets to the point that I can no longer ignore it with distractions, I tell myself these affirmations a few times.

I have handled this feeling before and I
can do it again.
I am safe.
This feeling will pass.
Anxiety cannot harm me.
Anxiety lies.
There is a time after this feeling when
things will feel okay again.
I will not feel like this forever.
I am as safe as I was an hour ago.
I have got this.

Crafting affirmations of your own will help, too,
because they can be quite personal. You might
be thinking, "I see affirmations all the time,
they aren't going to fix my anxiety," and I totally
understand that. It is true, these phrases will not
"fix" your anxiety. But what they *will* do is help
you talk to yourself with self-compassion and
self-belief—things you need a lot of when fighting
anxiety. Focus as much of your concentration on
those encouraging phrases. Whenever you have a
scary thought, or whenever your mind starts to say
"I can't," listen to that thought and oppose it with
an affirmation. For example:

Scary thought: What if something bad happens? I
can't do this, it's too hard.

**Encouraging affirmation:** I have handled this feeling before, I am safe, I can do this.

You don't have to believe the affirmation right away in order to tell it to yourself. I won't lie to you, it takes a lot of strength for it to work. When your mind is scared and telling you that something's going to go wrong, it feels almost stupid not to listen. But the thing is, anxiety is lying to you. By repeating these affirmations, you're reminding yourself that your anxiety is actually wrong, and you are safe.

While I was writing this book, I asked a few people if they wanted to talk about their experiences with some of the topics I discuss. The following quote is from Kayleigh Butler, a follower of The Positive Page, on her experience with low mood and anxiety:

> "I have struggled with anxiety and low mood for a number of years. Self-care has become very important and somewhat of a priority to me. I managed to get a job that was enough to pay the bills, but working in retail is demanding to say the least. One rude or impatient customer sticks in your memory and outweighs any good moments throughout the day. All it takes is one comment to put me

back in a low place and cause anxiety for the next day.

It's hard just getting out the door sometimes. I always look forward to coming home to my partner and switching off from work. I try very hard to separate work from home life. I always plan to do something I enjoy on my days off. I leave my phone on the bedside table and turn it off so that I can't be disturbed. I'll watch my favorite show and drink hot chocolate. I'll write and draw and bake.

My mood isn't consistently any particular way, it ebbs and flows like the sea. But doing a small thing each day for myself makes all the difference. Something that helps me is to remember a quote from Dr Brené Brown: 'Dare Greatly.' I dare greatly when I calmly deal with a difficult customer, I dare greatly when I stand up for myself, I dare greatly when I try a new way of getting to work when the routine doesn't go to plan. It's all the little victories that keep me going (and remembering that I can always ask my partner for help, no matter how ridiculous it seems). I let my struggles remind me of how strong I am and that I will make it through each day."

## CHAPTER 5

# When You're Anxious and Don't Know Why

Nothing's going to happen if you're anxious and can't work out why. It doesn't mean that there's something happening or going to happen that you should be scared of. It's not a warning, because anxiety cannot foresee the future. It's actually completely safe and okay to feel anxious, even if and when you don't know why. Anxiety cannot hurt you, you're not in danger, and this feeling will pass. You will feel safe again. Unexplained anxiety—that feeling of doom that just sits inside your chest all day without any obvious cause—can be really frustrating. Feeling anxious without any known reason can sometimes feel worse than when you do know why you're anxious, or do have a reason. When you know the cause, you can reassure yourself; when you don't, it can sometimes feel like there's no end to the anxiety. You may feel like you can't do anything about your anxious feelings simply because you don't know where they came from. However, just as they came on without reason, they can also go away on their own. You don't have to do anything anxiety tells you to do for the anxiety to pass. It will pass on its own in time.

In the meantime, healthy distractions can help you manage the feelings as they pass. I have to stress the importance of the word "healthy," as some people in this situation lean on unhealthy behaviors that then lead to larger problems. Unhealthy distractions won't help you in the long run, but healthy distractions actually could. Although engaging with distractions may seem like you're simply "ignoring" the problem, leaving the problem-solving for when you're feeling more stable is actually better than trying to do so in an anxious state.

Being able to successfully distract yourself from anxiety is quite a task to master, and it takes a lot of practice. It's important that, after you've felt anxious and are feeling more stable, you talk those feelings over with someone. Try to understand what's causing you to have periods of anxiety or panic attacks, and discuss how to handle them in the future.

Here are some ideas for healthy distractions that could help with your anxiety:

## Counting Colors

The good thing about this is that you can do it anywhere; all you need to do is to be able to look around you. Pick a color to start with, whichever one you like, and count how many things you can see that are that color around you. For example, I'm in my bedroom right now and see 15 white objects. If I have my phone and someone is around to chat, I often do this with them. I ask them to pick a color for me, and I reply back with a list of all the things I can see in that color.

## Reading

This one's pretty self-explanatory: read something. It can be a book, an eBook, a blog post, a (positive) Instagram post, or a magazine article (online or on paper if you have one!).

## Writing

This one's also pretty self-explanatory. I just had to include it, as it's one of my favorite methods. Not everyone enjoys writing, but for me, creative writing is a very effective way to manage my anxiety. When I write, I can zone into the feelings of a different character or person. This helps distract me from my anxiety, or from surroundings that are making me feel worried.

## Watching Something

You can watch the latest Netflix original or even just a 10-minute video on YouTube—anything that helps focus your attention away from your anxiety.

## Word Searches/Crosswords

This may sound a little random, but the process of having one word to look for in a bunch of letters helps focus my mind on one thing. That's why I carry a small word search book around with me.

## Tangle Toys/Handheld Puzzles

People like to use things like tangles, Rubik's Cubes, stress balls, and other sensory items to keep busy. For me, these sometimes include mini-maze puzzle toys or foldable rulers.

## Listening to Music or a Podcast

You can find some great podcasts out there about mental health. However, if you prefer to listen to something more light-hearted, you can find a comedy podcast or one on the topic of something you like to do!

## Going for a Walk or Exercising

This one comes with a few warnings: if you have a history of over-exercising, I wouldn't suggest doing this as a distraction. If you struggle with dissociation as part of your anxiety, I wouldn't go for a walk without bringing someone with you. However, for some, exercise can be a great distraction.

## Playing a Game with a Friend

You can play a video game to distract yourself if you want, but classic games can also be really help. I like to play card games with my brother, or anyone who's around to help distract me. I also like to play 20 Questions with my friends, which is something you can do from anywhere!

## Creating Art

Draw something or color something in! Some people find this more helpful than others, depending on their level of creativity.

\* \* \*

At the end of the day, no healthy distraction will totally fix your anxiety. What it will do is prevent you from developing *unhealthy* coping methods, and hopefully help the anxiety pass quickly. As I said, it's important to talk about how you feel, but if that's too hard to do when you're actually feeling it, then doing it afterwards is okay, too!

## CHAPTER 6

# When You're Anxious and Do Know Why

When you're worrying about something specific, it can take over your whole day and cause problems with your concentration, motivation, and enjoyment. To deal with this, a technique I like is scheduling "worry time." I set a time to deal with the worries I'm having and try not to engage with them at any other time in the day.

### SCHEDULING WORRY TIME

Setting a timeframe for worrying affirms the idea that the concerns I'm having will be dealt with properly, but also healthily, and won't take over my day! This can be done at any time of the day that suits you, and you can set it at the same time every day or at different times to fit your schedule. Every time you get a worry throughout the day, write it down as soon as you feel it. It can be big or small, and about anything. When you get to your scheduled worry time, you can read through all of your listed worries and deal with them one at a time. Often you'll find that, by the time you get to some of these worries, you don't actually need to do anything about them, as they have resolved themselves. Doing this exercise effectively can take a lot of practice. Shifting your focus away from the thing you're worried about or away from your feeling of anxiety is really (really, really) hard. Even if it feels like you're not doing it at 100 percent, it's still worth persisting and trying.

You can then interrupt your anxious thoughts by asking yourself the questions below. I find they help me challenge what the worrisome thoughts are trying to tell me. They help me connect back to what's happening in the present, rather than letting me focus on the hundreds of things I *think* are going to happen in a few hours, tomorrow, or next year. We have to learn to focus on the present and deal with life as it comes. Anxiety likes to live in the future, but the truth is, we can't actually see into the future. All anxiety does is make inaccurate guesses and scare us. If we can concentrate on what's actually happening right now, it may help us control the panic. Ask yourself these questions:

- Is what I'm anxious about happening right now, yes or no?

- Am in any physical danger, yes or no?

- 🗩 Is something going wrong right now, yes or no?

- 🗩 Is this feeling going to stay here forever and ever, yes or no?

If you answered no to most of the questions (and I hope you did!), then you're definitely going to be okay. You're safe without needing to do anything to make yourself more so. You don't need to be anxious, because you're not in danger! Sometimes our bodies think we're in danger when we aren't, and that's when the feeling of anxiety and all the symptoms that come with it kick in. If you can learn to reassure yourself by saying to your anxiety, "I don't need you, I'm okay on my own," and actually believing it, then you're so much closer to managing these feelings.

CHAPTER 7

# When You're Going into a Scary Situation

So right now, you're trying to challenge your anxiety. Thank you for being brave! I'll level with you: I know you don't want to put yourself in any type of scary situation. I know it feels like the most daunting and terrifying thing. You're probably thinking, "Why am I making myself do this? Why am I pushing myself to do something that makes me feel so anxious?" Just know that you're doing the right thing. Even if you feel anxious, it doesn't mean you're in danger or that anything "bad" or "unsafe" is going to happen. You are so brave, you can do this.

I know people say the phrase "You can do this!" a lot, but when you say it to yourself, try your best to actually believe it. When it already feels likely that something will go wrong, or that something bad will happen, anxiety makes that uneasy feeling 100 times worse. But remember, it's not true. When we ground ourselves, we understand that we're safe. You're capable of doing this scary thing, with or without anxiety. No matter what anxiety tells you, or how anxious you feel, you are capable. You don't have to be anxiety-free to feel safe. You don't have to be anxiety-free to do scary things. You don't have to know or feel 100 percent like you're going to be able to do it before doing it. It's okay to have uncertainties.

For me, when going out to do something that makes me afraid, the hardest part is leaving the house in the first place. It's a challenge to find the courage to get ready and not feel like I'm making a mistake or walking into danger. The truth is, leaving the house can feel like trying to run a marathon. You have to push yourself to find that brave mindset that claims, "No, anxiety will not rule my life, I can do this." You just have to get yourself out that door.

To do this, I take one step at a time, all the way until I'm at the location of said "scary situation." At the beginning, I used to cry pretty much every step of the way. But after doing this exercise enough times, after proving to myself that I could beat anxiety and do the scary things without anything bad happening, it got easier. The panic attacks slowed down, and I started being able to do scary things without crying about leaving the house. Putting myself in more anxious situations was terrifying, but little by little, it did eventually start to feel easier.

Here's an encouraging flow chart you can read when you're feeling anxious about leaving the house.

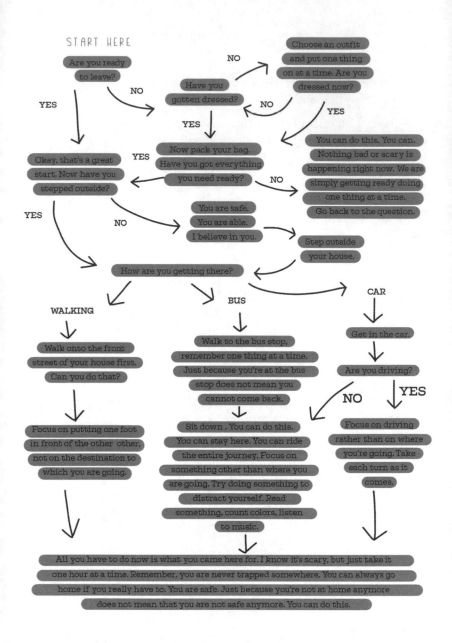

Often, people who have anxiety experience it in the same situation over and over again. For things like this, you may want to make a panic intervention plan. When you feel yourself starting to get anxious about going into one of your feared situations, you can read/answer the plan to help remind yourself that you can battle this feeling.

## PANIC INTERVENTION LIST

Use this list when you are trying to do something scary and you start having a panic attack.

### STEP 1: ANSWER THESE QUESTIONS

| Have you felt like this before? | Were you okay afterwards? | Have you been in this situation before? |
|---|---|---|
| Yes or No | Yes or No | Yes or No |

YOU WILL BE OKAY AGAIN.

### STEP 2: CHOOSE A HEALTHY COPING MECHANISM TO DEAL WITH THIS FEELING

♥ SAY SOME AFFIRMATIONS.

♥ TRY A GROUNDING METHOD.

♥ VISUALIZE (LIKE ACTUALLY VISUALIZE) IT GOING RIGHT, NOT WRONG!

♥ TALK TO SOMEONE ABOUT HOW YOU FEEL.

♥ BE GENTLE AND PATIENT WITH YOURSELF WHILE YOU BATTLE THIS FEELING.

**STEP 3:** LIST 3 REASONS WHY YOU WANT TO TRY PUTTING YOURSELF IN A FEARED SITUATION

♥

♥

♥

**STEP 4:** DESCRIBE HOW YOU WOULD FEEL IF YOU WERE BRAVE ENOUGH TO DO IT

_____

_____

_____

_____

**STEP 5:** LIST 3 AFFIRMATIONS THAT HELP YOU FEEL SAFE

♥

♥

♥

A common way to prevent panic is to use a grounding method. I have learned a lot of these in therapy. There are a few you can do—some you may have heard of before, some not!

## GROUNDING TRICKS

### Counting Colors

We covered this on page 57 where we discuss healthy distractions. Counting colors also works for grounding! Give it a try if you haven't already.

### Using Your 5 Senses

Find 5 things you can see, 4 things you can hear, 3 things you can touch, 2 things you can smell, and 1 thing you can taste. You can do this as many times as you like. You'll be surprised at how effective this is!

### Focusing on the Now

To do this, check yourself. Make sure you're not trying to predict the future or expecting a repetition of the past. Question if your thoughts are telling you that your anxious expectation is going to happen, even though we can't tell the future. Another way to do this is through meditation. You can listen to meditation music or do a guided meditation available on YouTube.

## Drawing It Out

Draw around your hand on a piece of paper (or just use your actual fingers if you don't have paper). On one finger, write something you did today—anything from getting dressed, to watching a show, to getting the bus. On the next finger, write something you're going to do tomorrow. If you have any plans, write those down; if not, it can be as simple as what you are going to have for breakfast, or what you're going to wear. On the next finger, write one word to describe how you're feeling right now. On the next one, write down what you *want* to feel right now, if you could choose any feeling at all. What feeling would you choose to feel right now? Would it be calm, happy, or just okay? On the last finger, write down something you can do to help you feel that desired emotion.

Below, a friend named Sandra has bravely shared her experience with anxiety and depression:

> I've suffered from depression, anxiety, and mental illness over the past twenty years, but in particular had a very bad experience of anxiety and my first ever panic attack a few years ago while I was unemployed.

It was the third time I had been unemployed and it lasted around 9 months. I was putting so much pressure on myself to have a "perfect job" and "perfect life" that I really suffered and struggled.

It was even harder as I'm a coach, consultant, and trainer with years of experience helping people with well-being, resilience, and mindset. I've had counseling various times and know all the tools. I stand up in front of rooms full of strangers and teach this stuff, but couldn't make it work for myself.

I felt like I wasn't myself and couldn't see a way out. I couldn't understand why it was happening. I shut myself away, couldn't leave the house. I became obsessed with trying to fix it.

My body would shake with fear from when I woke to when I slept. I was scared to go to sleep in case I didn't wake up. I ended up at the doctor's and emergency room numerous times as I had severe health anxiety and was convinced there was something seriously wrong and I was going to die.

I became physically ill and my mental health really suffered. I nearly checked myself into a mental health clinic as I was worried about what my brain would do. I never thought it would end.

I slowly started to reach out, do yoga, meditate (things that I never thought I would enjoy). I volunteered, had counseling, read self-help books, along with lots of other things, and some of these things were absolute lifesavers.

I'm not sure how, but I did eventually feel better. What I realized was, the more I tried to fix it and obsess, the worse it got. Not focusing on it and getting involved with other things was key.

I changed my mindset and have been running my own business for three years. I'm a Positive Mindset Coach and I help people silence their inner critic, embrace fear, and stop feeling like they're not good enough so they can live life with courage and on their own terms. I help people deal with anxiety, overwhelm, and self-doubt, empowering them to build self-belief and be more confident and resilient.

I now work with global organizations, have been a judge for The Learning Awards for the past three years, and have been featured as a guest speaker. I really can't believe how much my life has changed and improved by changing my thinking and looking after my well-being.

Your life can really change.

## CHAPTER 8

# When You've Just Had a Panic Attack

Don't beat yourself up for having a panic attack. Getting hit with anxiety is not your fault. If you're in a situation that's hard for you, be proud of yourself for trying! It's really great that you're trying to do that scary thing at all. If you weren't trying to battle a scary situation, but still had a panic attack, you should still be proud of yourself for getting through it. Things will slowly settle down inside your mind. This feeling will pass.

You've just been in a really intense state of mind and your body has just gone through high levels of stress, so it's a good idea to listen to your needs and prioritize them. You need to look after yourself. Go grab some water and sit out in some fresh air if you can. It's really important to stay hydrated after being in such a distressed state, but what's more important is that you don't follow your panic attack up with more negativity. If you feel guilty, stupid, or self-deprecating, then you need to practice self-compassion. Self-empathize and validate your feelings.

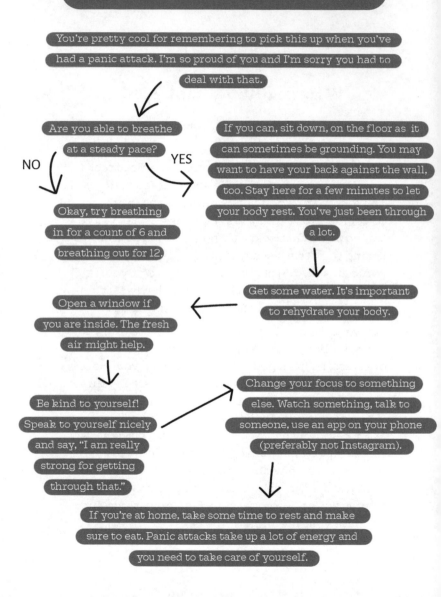

# POST-PANIC CARE FLOWCHART

You're pretty cool for remembering to pick this up when you've had a panic attack. I'm so proud of you and I'm sorry you had to deal with that.

Are you able to breathe at a steady pace?

**NO**

Okay, try breathing in for a count of 6 and breathing out for 12.

**YES**

If you can, sit down, on the floor as it can sometimes be grounding. You may want to have your back against the wall, too. Stay here for a few minutes to let your body rest. You've just been through a lot.

Get some water. It's important to rehydrate your body.

Open a window if you are inside. The fresh air might help.

Be kind to yourself! Speak to yourself nicely and say, "I am really strong for getting through that."

Change your focus to something else. Watch something, talk to someone, use an app on your phone (preferably not Instagram).

If you're at home, take some time to rest and make sure to eat. Panic attacks take up a lot of energy and you need to take care of yourself.

By this, I mean recognize just how much distress your mind has to be in to go into a panic. You may be used to it if you have panic attacks regularly, but this level of emotion is never easy to handle! No, you weren't being "stupid" or "pathetic"—your mind was simply struggling to process and fight off the fearful, controlling thoughts designed by your anxiety. That's a lot to deal with, so validate that experience within yourself. Take a second to let yourself know that the feelings you just had were hard, and that you did your best to deal with them.

Now, you need to forgive yourself. Rather than holding a grudge against yourself for having had a panic attack, remember that it's okay to panic. You weren't doing something wrong. You don't need to be angry at yourself for experiencing it. Choose acceptance and forgive yourself!

Don't forget that you can try again. We often feel like we've failed after experiencing this wave of fear, but it's okay to *not* always overcome anxiety— especially if you tried to put yourself in a new situation and it caused a panic attack. You can definitely try again. You can try to beat anxiety an endless amount of times. You don't have to have it all sorted out right away. Trying and trying with no results can drive you crazy, but I promise that you're getting closer with each attempt, even if it doesn't feel like it. You can do things at your own pace, and when you feel ready, you can try again. Below are some words from my friend Henry Garrett on his experience with anxiety:

> I experience anxiety as a barrier that prevents me from doing things I'd like to and as a painful, arduous battle that I'm forced to regularly partake in. Anxiety, for me, is the given name for my mind-body's oversensitive trigger to a stress response. I get stressed by things that I shouldn't get stressed by; or, more accurately, I get stressed by things that make it difficult to fit in with social expectations if you're stressed by them. One useful thing to learn if you're experiencing mental illness is to spot inappropriate "shoulds" and "shouldn'ts"; they'll be everywhere, carrying the weight of other people's expectations, as well as your own. But I do get stressed more than I would like to, and that stress causes me more pain than I would choose.

> Anxiety forced me out of my intended career, academia, and made it very difficult to imagine what else I could do. Anxiety also makes simple, everyday interactions feel like life-or-death challenges; it fills whole months with alternating terror and a sense that I'm a lazy failure. But anxiety has also forced me

to adapt, and taught me to duck and weave to find the path of least resistance. Adapting to mental illness is a balancing act—we can never tell which concessions we made were obstacles we may have found a way over. Perhaps, some of the things anxiety prevented me from doing were things I should have kept working at. But there's that 'should' again, and I'm happy with the life I'm building around the fights I no longer want to fight.

Questioning the force of "should" has helped me a lot. But so has an SSRI called Sertraline. Medication for mental illness holds a weird place in our society, and comparing that to the image of medication for "physical" illness is a good way to see that mental health stigma again—the notion that one "shouldn't" have to resort to medication for the mind. I don't want to paint antidepressants as a silver bullet, or ignore the side-effects that stop some people from using them, but I would like people to look closely at the reasons they have ambivalence toward them. Everything that people say can help—CBT, SSRIs, exercise, etc.—has helped me a little and put me a few paces closer to the relationship I'd like to have with stress. But as I move toward the place I should be, I'm also moving that "should" place closer to me, and that flexibility has allowed me to build a life I'm proud of.

## WORRY BOX: A CONSTANT PRESENCE

"This may sound silly: I hate feeling anxious and I always make my anxiety worse by thinking about it 24/7. It's 'what if my anxiety...' this and 'oh no, that will make me anxious...' that. I can't take my mind off it and it makes doing a lot of things harder."

Hi there. It sounds like you feel anxiety so frequently that you've begun to predict how you will react to and feel about different things. It's quite common for this to happen when people avoid situations that could maybe make them anxious. Struggling with this cycle of anxiety is really hard, but there is a way to break the loop. I strongly recommend, even though it's scary, to try and *not* avoid the things that make you anxious every single time. If you can, even if it's only once or twice to start, try to keep doing the things that make you anxious. This will prove to yourself that you can do it.

Something to remember when experiencing the "what if my anxiety..." thoughts is that, even with anxiety, you're still capable of doing hard things. Anxiety wants to make us feel that, when we're anxious, we can't do anything. Anxiety wants to control us. I'm here to tell you that it doesn't have to. You don't have to listen to what it says. Believe it or not, you can feel anxious and survive it—look how many times you've done it before! Try to challenge a "can't" thought with a counter "can" thought. Say to yourself, "So what if I do feel anxious? I am stronger than anxiety, I can survive this feeling." By doing this, you're empowering yourself and your capabilities, and *taking back* that power from your anxiety. I hope things get a lot better for you.

## WORRY BOX: ALWAYS ON THE CLOCK

"Hey, I am really struggling with my anxiety right now. There is a lot going on at school such as Christmas days, carol services, and a lot of end-of-topic assessments and exams. However, my anxiety seems to win every time. I don't get a day off where I haven't had a panic attack or an anxiety attack at some point about something that is happening, or has happened, or will happen. I don't know what to do."

Hello! It must be exhausting to have to deal with such high levels of anxiety with so little down time. Thank you for reaching out. It's not uncommon for people with anxiety to struggle when they have a lot of commitments! You're not alone there. Please try not to be hard on yourself. It's not your fault that you feel this way. Remember that anxiety cannot predict the future. It doesn't know that something *will* happen, but it likes to make you *think* it will by making you anxious.

If you can, try to take a day off when there are fewer things going on so you can relax and reset, because that's important, too. Then, when you feel like you have more energy, try to start working on your anxious thoughts. Do this with a therapist, counselor, or social worker, if you have one. If not, you can do this on your own or with a friend. It's good to try and identify the thoughts you experience when you're feeling anxious and decode what they mean to you. After doing this, you can reassure yourself that you're okay (because you are!), and you can let these thoughts come in and out without giving them any meaning or hold.

Anxious thoughts don't have to control you; they're just thoughts and they can't change, predict, or affect literally any part of your life. You can experience them and let them go without doing anything to "prevent" the scary thing they're making you think is going to happen. This is really difficult, but overcoming anxiety does take practice. Don't give up!

PART 3

# UNRAVELING
# YOUR STRESS

# WHAT WE DON'T NEED IN THE MIDST OF STRUGGLE IS SHAME FOR BEING HUMAN

-BRENÉ BROWN

## CHAPTER 9

# When You're Feeling Overwhelmed

You are only one person, with one mind and one body, and there's only a certain amount one person can take. You become overwhelmed when your mind takes on too many things at once and struggles to process them. This could be because you're busy or because your brain is already full—either way, the stress is likely to have built up and now everything is bubbling over.

When this happens, the most important thing to remember is that you don't have to do *anything* right this second. It's not healthy to keep pushing yourself when you're already at your limit, even if there's work that needs to be done by a deadline, or you just need to finish something that's stressing you out. Trying to do those things right away will only be more difficult.

At this moment in time, what you need to do is stop what you're doing. Stop working, talking, writing. Try your best to slow down the to-do list that's swirling around in your head. Depending on what's making you feel overwhelmed, this is sometimes very hard to do, and that's okay.

You can take out your journal or a piece of paper and write down everything that comes to your mind in the space of five minutes—everything from what you want for lunch, to what you are doing tomorrow. Get everything out in the open on paper. If your brain is full, you need to empty it, and this is the fastest way to do so. Once you've done this exercise, you may start to feel a little more relaxed. If not, take some time out, even if it's just half an hour. Do something calming for a little while—listen to music, watch a video, or go for a walk. Change the pace of your stressed body and mind by doing something slower.

If you're overwhelmed, not because of work or school, but from the symptoms of your mental health issues, writing lists in this way may not be as useful. That being said, it's still worth giving it a go to see if the change of pace eases your mind's anxious feelings. If that doesn't help, try identifying what symptoms are currently affecting you and thinking about how you can alleviate them to feel less overwhelmed. Learning to live with the symptoms more easily is something you can work on in therapy. Some of the things your mind could be doing that you may have missed are:

## OVERTHINKING

I know what you're thinking: "I overthink all the time and I know I'm doing it because I feel anxious." However, we sometimes don't realize just *how long* we've been overthinking something before we start to feel anxious. You may feel stressed because you're overanalyzing something (or more than one thing at once), and your mind is getting really tired trying to constantly resolve it. You may also be so used to overthinking that you don't even realize you're doing it. People with anxiety disorders overthink a lot of the time. Because the thought pattern is so normal to them, they don't realize how bad it is until they're mentally exhausted because their brain's been overworking all day long. If you struggle with overthinking and it's making you stressed and anxious, you may want to read the anxiety section of this book.

## PREDICTING THE FUTURE

When we have something important coming up in our lives, sometimes we spend a lot of time trying to predict what's going to happen. It's common for people with mental disorders to worry about changing something bad, stopping it from happening, or trying to control the situation. It's good to remember that we can't change the future.

We have no control over what is or isn't going to happen, and imagining every possible scenario takes up a huge amount of energy and space in our minds. **Learning to live in the present is practicing self-care.**

## COMPARING

Another thing that may be taking up a lot of your mental energy is comparison thinking. You may be in the habit of comparing anything of yours, such as success at work, lifestyle/possessions, looks, or even progress in recovery, to that of other people. Sometimes, wanting to be where someone else is at, or have what they have, or be able to do what they can do, makes it feel like we are failing. This constant comparison puts a lot of pressure on you to succeed, and is likely adding to your stress levels. Something to note is that you can't truly compare the aspects of your life to someone else's, because you have no way of knowing everything about them to make that comparison accurate. You can read more about this in the self-esteem section of the book.

An exercise you might want to try is dividing the things you're stressed about into what you can control and what you can't control. The following diagram can help with that. On each side, you can write anything from your worries, to thoughts on a certain topic, to problems you're currently facing—anything at all that's contributing to you feeling overwhelmed. For each point in the first column ("Things I Can Control"), come up with some viable solutions and make some decisions on what you want to do. Before you do this, you may want to make sure the problem is something that needs fixing, not just something you've been overthinking. For the second column ("Things I Can't Control"), you'll need to practice letting go of those problems and worries. Most worries we can't do anything about, and learning to sit with this reality is hard.

| THINGS I CAN CONTROL | THINGS I CAN'T CONTROL |
| --- | --- |
| | |

Another exercise I've done on more than one occasion, both with my therapist and on my own, is using a stress bucket. You may have seen this before in therapy; if you have, take this as a friendly reminder to use the technique right now if you're overwhelmed. If not, let me explain:

The stress bucket is another way of managing stressors in your life at the moment. Use the illustrations coming up in the next few pages to do this exercise.

For this exercise, you're going to fill the bucket up with everything that's currently affecting you. When I say everything, I mean every single stressor in your life at the moment—probably more than you realize! I'll guide you through the common ones first, step by step. Add each one to the stress bucket, and make the amount of space each one takes up different depending on how much it's affecting you at the moment.

1.  Start with everyday stress, the basic functions we do each day: get up, get dressed, shower, eat, walk, drive, talk to people. These are things that everyone does, but they still need to go into the bucket. You might think they don't count because they're not causing you stress. But think about it: when someone's going through a really hard time, what are common things they find difficult? Sleeping, eating, and showering are things that spring to mind. Everything counts, even if it's small.

2.  Next is relationship stress. When I say this, I don't just mean romantic relationships, I mean every single relationship in your life— friends, family, partners, they all count. For now, this is just general relationship stress. If something specific happened, like a break up,

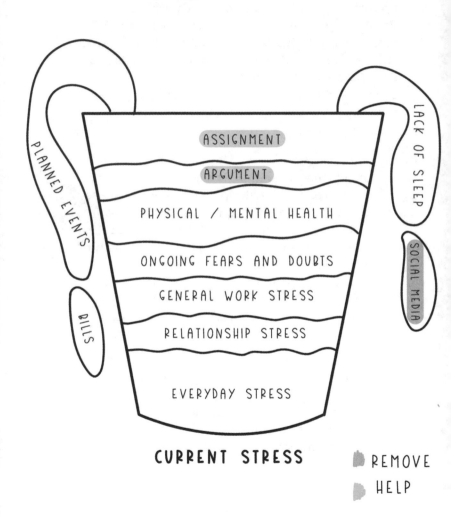

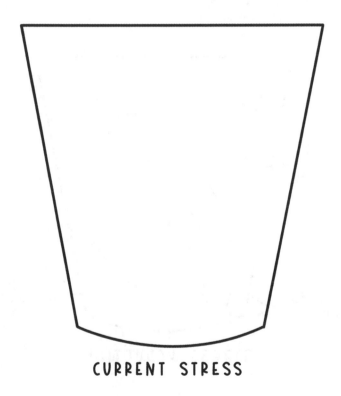

STRESS BUCKET

CURRENT STRESS

# STRESS BUCKET EXAMPLE

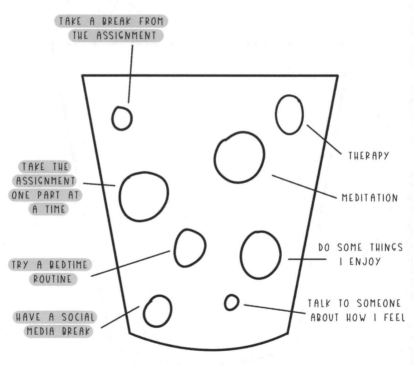

TAKE A BREAK FROM THE ASSIGNMENT

TAKE THE ASSIGNMENT ONE PART AT A TIME

TRY A BEDTIME ROUTINE

HAVE A SOCIAL MEDIA BREAK

THERAPY

MEDITATION

DO SOME THINGS I ENJOY

TALK TO SOMEONE ABOUT HOW I FEEL

## STRESS REDUCTION

STRESS REDUCTION

or an argument, or the loss of a friend, you can note that later.

3. Next is general work stress. This just the act of going to work (or school) and everything that involves.

4. Next are ongoing fears and doubts. These are interesting to me because, even though I have fears that stem from my anxiety, I also have more general fears. Those belong in this section. Here's a good example: I fear I'll never be able to buy a house because they're so expensive! This fear isn't connected to my disorder, it's just a general life doubt that comes to my mind some days more than others.

5. Next is health. If you have any physical or mental illnesses/disorders/injuries, then this one may probably feel pretty big!

6. Now that we've noted all the non-specific things, we now note everything that is either specific to you or to the time you currently in. This just means anything—situation, task, event, piece of work, thought, person, behavior, etc.—that is causing you difficulty. Once you run out of room in the cup, draw

these things as overflow. If you're confused, look at the example.

The bucket on the opposite side is for stress reduction.

1. If there are any stressors in your **current stress** bucket that you can remove from your life, even if only temporarily (like for a week or so), highlight them. These are highlighted in blue in the example.

2. If there are some stressors that you can't take out completely, get another highlighter and mark those you *can* try to do something about/help yourself with. In the example, these are highlighted in yellow.

3. Each highlighted stressor you try to help alleviate will punch a hole in your full bucket. Label the holes in the stress bucket with the activities you complete.

4. Repeat this, adding as many mechanisms you can to help with your stressors.

After that, we're going to add other things that can help reduce stress, and in turn add more holes to the bucket. For some people these could be therapy, meditation, talking to friends, or going for a run. Often this involves doing things you enjoy, something creative, watching movies, reading. The reasons for doing this exercise are:

1. You can see that your stress isn't coming out of nowhere!

2. You can see what your bigger stressors are.

3. You can reflect on potential ways to decrease your current level of stress.

4. You can think of ways to tackle some of your stressors, maybe even ones you've tried before, and go back to look at the sheet when you start feeling overwhelmed.

5. Writing down things you enjoy reminds you to add these things into your life, so you're not just doing stressful things all the time. Often, enjoyment (if you can find it through all the stress) is a natural de-stressor, even if it's only temporary.

## CHAPTER 10

# When You're Really Busy

Seeing as you're really busy, I'll keep this chapter short.

There are only so many hours in a day, and therefore, you can only do a certain amount of things each day. If you're really busy and it's causing you more stress than you can handle, recognize that you may be taking on too much. If you've been experiencing high levels of stress recently, you may want to assess your options to see if there's anything you can take out of your schedule, or if there's something you can share responsibility of with someone else. If you can't, the other option would be to delegate efficiently. Something I find really helpful when I'm struggling with this is making a schedule. It might sound obvious, but let me explain.

I used to write lists. Every day I would get up and write a list of all the things I needed to do, and then I'd spend the entire day beating myself up for not getting everything done. This caused me a lot of anxiety, and I'd feel guilty for not getting "enough" things accomplished. Most of the time, when I feel guilty, I also feel anxious. This causes my productivity to decrease, as I can't concentrate. Here's how scheduling has really helped me: Every Monday (but not actually every Monday of the year, I'm not a machine and I have days with no motivation, too!), I write a to-do list as I normally would. But now, I write out every day of the week and spread the tasks across the week, delegating just a few tasks to each day that I need to get done. This makes things feel a lot easier.

Before this, I expected to get as *much* done as humanly possible every single day, and that's just not realistic. You have to set goals for yourself that you can actually achieve each day. Otherwise, you're going to feel like you're not achieving enough, even when you are! I like to tick off these tasks as I complete them; most days, I have around three to four that I need to get done, but some days I have lots of smaller tasks. This usually helps motivate you. For example, rather than writing "tidy the house" on your to-do list, write each task individually, like this: "vacuum the floor," "run the dishwasher," "do laundry," etc. Tick each off as you do them, and you'll realize that you're doing more than you think. Another example could be, instead of writing "do homework/coursework," you can more specifically put "start writing the essay," or "make an essay plan."

To begin, I'd suggest writing everything down on one long list, putting the things that are of the highest priority on the first days of your schedule. Also, group together tasks that make sense to do on the same day—being organized in this way could save you time. Scheduling properly has saved me time because before, I'd waste time being stressed and nothing would get done, as my energy was being taken up by feelings. Some days this still gets to me, but grounding myself back to the realistic expectations of my schedule and my achievable goals helps me. Please remember to not expect too much of yourself—you can't always magically get everything done in one day!

Oh, and when you're working, remember that you don't feel the same way every day. If you're wondering why you might be finding something more difficult than you normally would, it could be because you're in a bad headspace at the moment. This is okay. You don't have to feel wonderful, be super productive, and win every single day. You're only human!

## CHAPTER 11

# When You're Stressed about School/Exams

## RETHINKING EXAMS

Take this as your friendly reminder that exams do not define your worth. Academic achievement is not the only type of success or mark of intelligence in your life. I promise you, the results you get for your school work do not, and never will, dictate 100 percent of how your life will turn out.

I know it can feel overwhelming when you have a lot to get done, especially for an essay or an exam. You may worry about not having revised as much as you wanted and as a result, you feel underprepared. But remember this: you've spent so much of your life preparing for exams, so when you feel *unprepared*, you're likely not taking into consideration the many life skills you overlook each day. There's an entire list of things you've learned to do to be able to even sit through an exam in the first place. To be able to take an exam or write an essay, you use writing, reading, and memory skills—and if you're reading this, it's likely that you're using all of these skills at the same time. You also manage your mental health, stress levels, and nerves.

So before being hard on yourself about academic achievement, remember exactly how much you're doing, because it is a lot. For your own sanity, please don't put too much pressure on yourself. You can only do your best, and that's enough; you can't expect any more than that. **Focus on how hard you are trying, not how much you are succeeding.** It's not always about the end result. That might sound cliché, but if you think about it, you've still learned all of the topics presented in your classes. You've attended, listened, and learned—even if you don't get a top grade for that, you've still accomplished something. You've still tried your best, and that cannot be dismissed just because you didn't get the grade you wanted. It's so important to give yourself credit for your hard work, no matter the outcome.

Let's start now. To help you do this, use this empty bullet point list. Here, you can write down everything you've accomplished and the skills you've acquired since you first started school to prepare for your current exams.

## I HAVE...

- ♥
- ♥
- ♥
- ♥
- ♥
- ♥
- ♥
- ♥
- ♥
- ♥
- ♥
- ♥
- ♥
- ♥
- ♥
- ♥
- ♥
- ♥

When you're working, please remember to take a break. If it's all too much and it feels like you're drowning in work, papers, and coursework, take it one hour at a time, or even one task at a time. You'll still make it through the exam period or area of work that you're currently finding difficult. You'll feel less stressed again. It's going to be okay, I believe in you, and you should feel proud of whatever grade you get because you're trying your hardest, and that will always be enough.

## SCHOOLING YOURSELF AND OTHERS

Exams and coursework aren't the only stressful parts of school. All that aside, school itself can be really stressful. The social aspect, the routine, the deadlines, the pressure—it's a lot to process each day. If any part of school is affecting you negatively, then you need to tell someone. You don't have to struggle alone. If there's a problem and you can't think of a solution yourself, it's good to find someone who can help you find one. That being said, if the problem is that your mental health is making school harder, there may not be a perfect "solution." There are things you can do, though, to make your experience a bit easier.

When I was in elementary, middle, and high school, not only was I really shy, but I was experiencing symptoms of my anxiety disorders without having any understanding of them at all. This made school stressful for me, especially on days when I was unable to concentrate on a lesson because I was fighting off a panic attack. When I look back at myself during that time, I can't believe how much resilience I had, sitting in those classes despite my mind trying to spontaneously combust. My friends helped me as much as they could, which I was always grateful for. But the thing that gets me is, if there was simply better education on mental health when I was at school, things could have been easier. The teachers were aware of my situation to some extent, and I was seeing the school counselor, but the atmosphere they created felt very "hush hush"—as if struggling with my mental health wasn't something people wanted to talk to me about.

Things changed a little bit in my last year of high school, when I became part of a few groups that addressed coping with exam stress and self-confidence. What the teachers didn't understand was that I wasn't just suffering from exam stress, I was also trying to work out how to live with a mental disorder—two very different things. This misunderstanding was the direct result of a lack of awareness, something that sparked my desire to start The Positive Page and educate people as much as I could.

Once I got to college and had a better understanding of my own mind, I was in a better position to explain to my teachers how my disorders affect me. I made it my mission to have an open discussion with them, and we made an agreement that, if I was feeling anxious or having a panic attack, I could leave the lesson to try and calm down. I highly recommend speaking to your teachers about this if you also think this will be helpful. For me, it took a lot of pressure off just knowing I could escape without someone being angry at me or needing an explanation. That is my biggest tip when it comes to school and mental disorders: talk to people about what you're going through. It is *not* a shameful thing to be diagnosed with a mental illness. It is not a shameful thing to be going through a difficult time. If you need help on how to talk about your mental health, revisit part 1 of this book.

## CHAPTER 12

# When You're Stressed about Work

It's easy to forget that life's not all about work. We've grown up in a society that, for the most part, measures a person's worth by how much they work and how productive they are. This mindset disregards other aspects of a person's life. I don't know what "work" is for you, but I do know that if you're reading this section of the book, then it's likely causing you problems. This could be helped by reconnecting with the things you enjoy. It's common for people to get so wrapped up in their work routines that they forget having fun is important, too.

Some people feel guilty when they're told they haven't worked "enough," because they think that means they're lazy. I think this is because, from an early age, we're taught that work equals good, and fun is only possible once you've done enough work. From homework to exams, we're living a life in preparation of eventual work as adults, so it's no wonder we forget the importance of fun in the process.

A balance of work and fun is healthy, but often, a lot of people go really far in one direction. They spend all day, every day doing nothing but work. Not only is this physically and mentally draining, but it ignores the other parts of your natural emotional needs as a human. So if you're feeling stressed, it could be because you're out of balance in this respect and not tending to your other needs. I know sometimes it's easier said than done, but find some time in your week to *just have fun*. Do something you enjoy that lifts you up, that you're passionate about, on a regular basis. You deserve to relax, too.

Reserving time for yourself doesn't make you lazy. Having fun (or even doing a little bit of nothing) is a good thing. Healthy minds need breaks!

In these breaks and time for enjoyment, you could:

## LEARN A NEW SKILL

This can be so fun and nowadays, the internet makes it a lot easier! Your new skill could be a creative one, like some kind of art, drawing, graphic design, or photography. It could be a new language. It could be something outside, like gardening (or even learning about house plants if you don't have a garden), learning how to use a compass, or going on a hike. You could even combine some together: go hiking outside, collect some leaves or twigs, and make art or photograph them. Let your imagination out for a while, rather than trying to turn it off and concentrate at work. A few years ago, my mom started learning to do pottery. After work a few times a month, she would go to her pottery class and come back smiling. It made me really happy to see her spend time on something she enjoyed.

## PICK UP A NEW HOBBY OR RECONNECT WITH AN OLD ONE

Did you ever give up on something just because you stopped having the time to do it? Do you miss it? Now that you're making more time for yourself, it might be the time to try it again. Things that come to mind are dancing, reading (you could join a book club!), journaling, sewing, photography, or sports.

## MEET UP WITH A FRIEND OR FAMILY MEMBER

Sometimes we just need to reconnect with the people we love.

## DO SOMETHING RELAXING

Meditation, yoga, massages, aromatherapy, cloud watching, writing affirmations—do anything that might help you focus on something other than work for a while.

## WORRY BOX: BATTLING COMPULSIONS

"Recently I've been experiencing feelings of stress and anxiety more often than usual, sometimes even panic attacks, and have been carrying out compulsions more frequently and getting more stressed about doing them. Sometimes I feel everything all at once, sometimes I feel nothing at all. I spoke to someone at school about this and have been put on the waiting list to talk to a school guidance counselor. I asked for my parents not to be informed. I don't know how long the wait will be and I don't know how to handle my feelings in the meantime, as I feel I have no one to talk to. Any advice?"

Hello, I'm sorry things are so stressful for you. Compulsions are one of the hardest things to break, I completely understand why this is having such a big impact on you. It's really good that you've reached out to both me and a guidance counselor. These are big steps, and you should be proud of yourself. It sounds like you have a lot of feelings floating around and that can be quite overwhelming. Be gentle with yourself at this time, it's not easy. In the times where you're "feeling all the feelings" at once, try to pause what you're doing and write down some of these thoughts. Getting them down on paper could help declutter your mind. You could even write a list of compulsions you're doing, which will help when you see a counselor. Keep going, you can get through this.

## WORRY BOX: DISSOCIATIVE EPISODE

"I experienced a dissociative episode last night for the first time and I'm not sure how I feel today. I have been feeling depressed, anxious, and a bit lost recently, but then my whole body just got numb. How do I help myself when this happens and what can I do to feel normal again after a dissociative episode?"

I am so sorry you've had to deal with dissociation. It's scary, but I am so glad you reached out. Dissociation occurs either in response to trauma, or upon being overwhelmed with thoughts and feelings you're unable to process. That's why, for some dissociative disorders, you start to feel numb and your mind feels kind of airy. If this is the case for you, it's important to keep yourself safe when you dissociate; sometimes you can do things that are dangerous, as you're not fully concentrating. I would advise you to look up some grounding techniques to do when you start to feel your mind dissociating. Reaching out to someone and talking to them, even if it's just about the weather, can help you to stay grounded. Some other techniques are sitting on the floor, running your hand under water (not hot water!), and drawing.

Feeling normal again after dissociating is hard; things can feel blurry, and that can make you feel anxious. My best advice is, if it happens at night, sleep it off; if it happens during the day, try your best to do something you normally would. Do something to remind yourself that you are safe and that the day is okay—just as okay as it was before you dissociated. I hope that you're okay. These symptoms are difficult to deal with, but remember you're not alone.

I asked my friend Abigail if she'd share her experience dealing with stress, and this is what she said:

> Stress impacts all of us in different ways. I found that heading off to college was a big trigger for me—being in a new city, with new people, and studying a subject I hadn't learned about before. As someone who didn't drink or party, I found freshman week to be particularly difficult and my panic attacks got worse. However, I needn't have worried because I met some of my best friends within a few months and soon settled in.

I tried a variety of coping mechanisms to manage stress throughout my time in college, but the ones that worked best for me were:

- ◉ Going for a walk. Probably the simplest thing to do, but definitely the most beneficial, especially with a friend or a new album to listen to. Taking half an hour out of my day, in whatever weather, really helps to clear my head.
- ◉ Talking to my professors. Making sure they were all aware of my anxiety and stress meant that they had no issue if I felt I had to leave a lecture or couldn't come in one day. They were all super understanding and a great support network to have.
- ◉ Finding a safe space on campus where I could spend time alone to rest or get away.
- ◉ And just making sure I kept as organized as possible. Generally, schedules written in colorful pens with doodles cheered me up when looking at them. Planning and being prepared the best I could allowed me to take time away to enjoy myself and all my new experiences.

# PART 4

# RIDING THE STORMY WAVES

YOU WILL MAKE IT THROUGH THE STORMY WAVES

CHAPTER 13

# When You're Feeling Low

It's okay to cry. It's okay to feel low. You're not alone in this darkness, and I promise it won't last forever. You don't have to try and force yourself to feel happiness. The feelings you have at the moment are valid, too, even if you don't know why you're feeling them. If you can, please try not to get angry at your low mood. I know it's frustrating, but you deserve to be spoken to gently, not with hate and self-judgement. Give yourself a break.

The most important thing to do when you're feeling low is to not isolate yourself. It's so common for people to sit and fight with their thoughts all on their own. It's so easy for a low mood to cut you off from everything and everyone you love because the days seem so long and painful, and you feel the people around you may not understand. When you isolate yourself, however, you're depriving your mind of human connection and understanding.

If you have a friend or family member that you can talk to about how you feel, that's amazing. It may not fix how you feel right away, but talking to them is much better than trying to deal with it alone. However, being with someone doesn't mean you *have* to talk about how you feel. If the thought of that is overwhelming, it's okay to meet up with someone and just talk about anything, even if it has nothing to do with your mental health. Having people to spend time with, and knowing that you're not alone, is beyond comforting. Interrupt your low thoughts with discussions about the little things with your friends or family.

Something that helps me when I'm feeling low is practicing acceptance. This might sound like a strange suggestion, but when I'm feeling a large amount of any emotion, my first instinct is to try to fix it or find some way to control how I feel. What I have learned about life, however, is that it's not about controlling feelings and emotions—it's about controlling how you respond to them. Bear with me, because I know this is a million times harder to put into practice. Emotions, both good and bad, are part of the human experience, and whether we like it or not, we *will* still experience the negative ones no matter how much we try to control them. These feelings will come up regularly and you will *have* to feel them, especially if you have depression or another mental illness. And I don't know about you, but I tend to get stressed when I try to stop myself from feeling these emotions. They're scary and feel really bad, so surely trying to control them is the most logical thing, right? Every time I try, though, this ends up making me feel *more* anxious. I end up feeling worse about myself because I feel like I'm fighting a losing battle.

Waking up and telling yourself to try to be happy, to not be upset, to not feel low about something, to not sink to this low place again—when you do this, you're fighting *against* yourself rather than working *with* yourself. Think of it like this: if your friend told you they were feeling really low, you wouldn't respond with, "Well, just *stop* feeling low." So why do it to yourself? Instead of trying to control emotions that are uncomfortable (really, really uncomfortable), try to control *how you act* in response to these emotions.

Next time you're feeling down, try just listening to what you're feeling, if only for a moment. Understand the emotions. They might be uncomfortable for a while, but you can handle them. Practice accepting what you cannot control. The next phase is not engaging with things that could make them worse in the long run, like substance abuse, negative self-talk, or self-isolation. At this time, you need support and kindness; try to intervene by talking to yourself nicely and accepting that feeling low is okay.

Though it might be here for a little while, the low mood *will* go away.

So again, reach out to someone so you know you're not alone. Try your best not to get mad at yourself for feeling depressed because it's not your fault. You cannot always control how you feel and you don't deserve any form of punishment, even self-admonishment. Managing this dark feeling makes you so, so brave, and I'm really proud of you for enduring it. If I could take it away I would, but you *can* do scary things. You can battle upsetting feelings. You are stronger than you think.

A brave soul on my page was kind enough to anonymously share her experience with low mood:

> I know a low mood can be hard to get out of, but I have learned to be patient with myself, let myself feel emotional or low for a few days or weeks, and then start thinking of ways to feel better. Comfort things help, like listening to uplifting music, funny audiobooks, or just having a long soak in the bath.

> I then write down everything I have achieved from the last few years and reflect on happy times, which usually gets me feeling a little better. Surrounding yourself with good people helps, too, as they can help lift your spirits and make you laugh/smile, but also understand

what you're going through and give you the
space you need.

## CHAPTER 14

# When You're Feeling Unmotivated

One of the most frustrating feelings is wanting motivation but not being able to find it. I understand that struggle. Sometimes you just really need to get something done, but can't find anything to push you to do it. If you're feeling this way right now, I would first like to remind you to not put too much pressure on yourself. It's important that you're not too hard on yourself in these moments. Instead, reflect on how you've been feeling today, or this week, and take some time to check in.

- ◉ Has your mind been overworking?
- ◉ Have you been stressed, anxious, or low?
- ◉ Are you battling a lot of self-doubt?

While you're doing this, it's good to also check in on other aspects of your well-being that may be affecting you today.

- ◉ Did you sleep well?

- Have you given yourself enough breaks and downtime?
- Are you eating properly?

Sometimes we don't have the motivation to do something because we're having issues with our mental health. Don't just assume you're just being lazy or making excuses before kindly checking in with yourself. If you're feeling low or anxious, or your brain has been working at full steam for days, then it's likely to take up a lot of your energy and concentration. There's usually an underlying reason for feeling unmotivated. For me, it's often self-doubt. Most times, I become unmotivated when I start feeling like what I'm doing/making/ planning isn't good enough, or that I'm not going to be able to do it. I'll let you in on a secret: while writing this book, at just about every chapter there was a point where I lost motivation because of this exact reason!

I don't know what task you're trying to complete— maybe it's a project or presentation for work, maybe it's coursework or an essay for school, maybe it's artwork. Maybe you've lost motivation to do anything at all. Life can seem like it's made up of a whole load of things you don't want to do. I'm pretty sure there has to be a reason you're feeling this way, though, and I won't accept you thinking you're just being lazy as an excuse. If you're having a rocky patch with your mental health, your motivation is going to be affected. That's just how it works!

Once you've worked out why you're feeling unmotivated, you then need to *find something you can do about it*. If the problem is physical (sleeping, eating, having down time, etc.), then it may be worth trying to adjust those things before you start what you need to do. Go to bed early, eat at proper meal times, and plan breaks into your schedule. If your emotions are affecting you, then it's probably best to wait until a time when these feelings have passed. However, if this is a regular problem, that might be difficult.

If you lack motivation for similar or the same tasks each week, then it's definitely worth working through the underlying problem to find your motivation again. As I said before, for me, it was a lack of self-belief. I sometimes go through weeks where I lose self-confidence, and that makes completing my work particularly hard. With my therapist, I recognized that I was feeling unmotivated because I didn't think I could do my work well enough. After we identified the cause to be self-doubt not facts, I was then able to give myself a break. It helped me stop getting frustrated with myself for not working as quickly or as soundly as I wanted. Instead, it made me mindful of the fact that, if work was feeling more difficult than usual, it could be because of my mental state. Now that I know this, I try to manage these days by talking to myself with kindness, rather than with judgement. Some days it's harder to keep up than others. Self-love is a journey, after all.

When you feel unmotivated, how do you talk to yourself? Do you internally shout at yourself? Do you start ordering instructions for what you need to do today, and when you need to do it? Do you get frustrated and use a judgmental tone if you haven't done everything yet? If you do, you're likely making it *worse*.

A good way to check this is to ask if you'd talk to a friend like this. Would you be mean to them in order to try and get them to do something? No. So why treat yourself that way? Instead of coming at yourself with anger, replace it with kindness. Be conscious of your own feelings and situation. Be understanding of the fact that you're finding it hard today, and that that's okay. Because it is okay to have times when work just feels impossible. Rather than demand productivity, reassure yourself gently. Below, you can fill in a grid with your unhelpful voice and replace it with a more positive one.

# GENTLE MOTIVATION

Find motivation by being patient with yourself
rather than frustrated.

## FRUSTRATED VOICE

"You have to do this today, no excuses, and the fact that
you haven't done it yet is really irresponsible."

## PATIENT VOICE

VS.

"Take it little by little, it's okay that it's difficult. Try your best—that's all
you can do. You can always try again when you're feeling better."

## FRUSTRATED VOICE

## PATIENT VOICE

VS.

## FRUSTRATED VOICE

## PATIENT VOICE

VS.

## MOTIVATION FINDER

Another way to refuel your motivation is to remember why you're doing something in the first place. Even the most common of tasks, like getting dressed or making lunch, have reasons behind them. By doing this, you're giving your efforts purpose. For everyday tasks, here are some reasons why you might have wanted to do them in the first place:

## GETTING DRESSED

Simply getting dressed helps you feel more confident and readier for the day. Pick out an outfit you love to achieve something you've been finding difficult lately, to go see a friend, or to go for a walk.

## MAKING A MEAL (OR A SNACK!)

To fuel your body, to get some energy, to prepare for the day's work, to practice your cooking skills, to try something new, or to face a fear and feel proud of yourself (if you struggle with eating).

## TIDYING YOUR SPACE

To have a more organized space in which to work/live, to declutter (which helps with de-stressing), to simply have the satisfaction of a tidy space (yes, some people love this!).

Now it's your turn! Fill in the diagram on the next page with your own tasks.

# REMEMBERING WHY: FOR EVERYDAY TASKS

Fill in this page with everyday tasks and why you want to do them.

Task:

Reason you're doing it:

Task:

Reason you're doing it:

Task:

Reason you're doing it:

Task:

Reason you're doing it:

Task:

Reason you're doing it:

If you're not feeling unmotivated to do everyday tasks, and are instead having trouble with more specific or long-term tasks and projects, then its best to make your own list with your own reasons. Here are some more generic examples you could take and personalize:

## COMPLETING SCHOOL WORK

To get ahead of your schoolwork so you don't have to think about it anymore, to turn in your homework on time and avoid the stress of not having it done, to improve your knowledge, to get better at the subject, to tick something off your to-do list.

## COMPLETING A PERSONAL PROJECT

To make something you're proud of, to impress the person you're making it for, to better your ability to do the work, to learn or teach.

## CREATING ARTWORK

To improve your technique, to put the art on your wall, to create something you're proud of, to express yourself, to find new ways of making art, to make something for someone else.

# FINDING MOTIVATION FOR PROJECTS

Fill in this page with long-term projects and why you want to do them.

Project:

Reason you're doing it:


Project:

Reason you're doing it:


Project:

Reason you're doing it:


Project:

Reason you're doing it:


Project:

Reason you're doing it:

Hopefully, there's something in this chapter that will help with your lack of motivation. It's a good sign in itself that you've just finished reading and are trying hard to find motivation. Maybe you have more motivation than you think! Maybe you *can* actually do it. Maybe you just need to believe in yourself some more.

CHAPTER 15

# When You're Feeling Stuck

Feeling stuck? This alone can dip your mood or cause a lot of tension in your everyday mindset. The dissatisfied feeling of not moving forward can also add confusion to your understanding of what you want in life. We might not realize it, but we think a lot about what we want and what our plans are.

You might feel stuck because you're unhappy with the way your life is at the moment, and aren't sure of what next step to take. This can be caused by anything: work, career, relationships, living situation, the future. Do you know what you feel stuck about? If you do, that's great! That's the first step toward becoming unstuck! If not, let's break this feeling down into smaller parts. Write down the different aspects of your life in the following diagram.

# BECOMING UNSTUCK

Fill in the columns.

| | Name of task/part of your life | How do you feel about it? | Can it be changed if needed? |
|---|---|---|---|

Now take a look at what you've filled in. What parts are making you unhappy? Is there any aspect of your life that you can take out because of this? Perhaps there's even a person bringing you down that you shouldn't spend time with anymore. Is there anything that you can alter to make your life more enjoyable? You might find that you'll start to feel happier just by changing something really small.

Sometimes we feel stuck, not because we need to take someone or something out of our lives, but because we just need to *wait* for something to happen. This can make you experience a lot of discomfort. Not knowing why things don't feel right or what you're missing can bring a lot of feelings to the surface, and we often don't know what to do with them. Sometimes, though, we just have to sit with them and wait for change to come to us. However, if you're feeling like you can't do that, go out and look for change. Try new things. Begin a new activity you've not done before, meet new people, learn a new skill. Here is a list of some things you could try:

- Baking
- Photography
- Joining a book club
- Going to a party

- Volunteering at a charity, animal shelter, or youth center
- Trying a new sport or exercise

## WHEN YOUR DIAGNOSIS IS STANDING IN YOUR WAY

If you have any type of mental illness, the effects of that condition (be they physical or mental) are likely to make you feel stuck at some point. It's very common for this feeling of "stuckness" to come when you've lost hope. Along with overwhelming emotions, symptoms that are likely to keep you stuck on a hopeless loop are behavioral problems that get in the way of your everyday life. These can be anything from:

- **Safety behaviors.** These are most common in people with anxiety disorders, and can include avoidance, reassurance, unhealthy distractions, and escaping.
- **Unhealthy coping mechanisms,** like substance abuse, isolation, and oversleeping.
- **Compulsions.** These are most common in people with OCD, and include things like checking, rituals, correcting thoughts, reassurance, and repetitive behaviors.
- **Disordered eating.**

These behavioral symptoms are by far the most difficult things to deal with, as they affect your life in such a destructive way. They're also the most difficult things I discuss in this book.

You probably feel like these behaviors dictate everything you do. I know that in my case, I didn't realize just *how many* compulsions and safety behaviors I was doing on a daily basis that made my anxiety worse until I got to therapy. They became almost "normal" in my routine to help me feel safe. The more I developed them, the worse my anxiety and OCD got. The worse those got, the lower I would feel. Every time I couldn't do something because of these, I would feel bad about myself, my life, and my future. These behaviors and thoughts that came with them made me sink so low, I thought I wouldn't recover.

I truly felt stuck, and I thought that would last forever. But I'm very proud to say that, as I write this, I no longer hold that belief. I know that I can "manage" the symptoms of my OCD and health anxiety, including the safety behaviors that come from them. You can do this, too. You're capable of being brave, challenging unhealthy behaviors, and breaking the loop. You're capable of changing something that you do because of an illness that is bad for your well-being. But I'm not going to lie to you, making this type of change is really, really,

*really* hard. It will not happen overnight, and just because you decide you want to change it doesn't mean it'll just happen.

To get unstuck in this way requires a lot of effort. It's scary, it will take a lot of practice, and there will most likely be a lot of unsuccessful attempts along the way. But just because you don't succeed straight away doesn't mean you can't do it. No matter how many times you try and fail, no matter how many times it feels too hard, it doesn't mean you won't ever be able to do it. You *can* make a change in behavior. I promise, you don't need your safety behaviors, compulsions, or whatever your disorder tells you to do. You don't need them. You don't need to isolate yourself, or avoid the people and things you love. You don't need to hide yourself away. You can fight back.

If you make a change as difficult as this, then you might start to do things more easily than before. In some cases, you'll be able to do things that you couldn't do at all. If you do make a change, or even try your best to, I'm so proud of you. You should be unbelievably proud of yourself for trying, too, because it's hard and takes a lot of courage.

## CHAPTER 16

# When You're Feeling Empty

Just because you feel empty doesn't mean your life is empty. When we feel low, numb, or even lost, we often look at ourselves and the things in our lives and think that there's nothing meaningful there. You might be walking around feeling like a piece of cardboard—flat, dull, and easily breakable. This numbness may fill your day, or even your week, and I know you're wishing something would come along to make you feel better. I hope you're not losing hope. It probably gets tedious, listening to people say this, but I'm going to say it anyway as you might need to hear it. This horrible feeling of emptiness will not stay forever. Just because it's here now doesn't mean it'll still be here this time next week, or even this time tomorrow. I know reading this won't necessarily cure you, but it's important to remember that the numb feeling is not permanent, and you *will* feel excited, happy, and proud again.

Now, I don't know what caused this numb feeling— maybe you don't even know, which is okay, too. I do know that you're still capable of feeling all the feelings. Even if you can't see your purpose in life right now, you belong here. Your life is important. Your life has meaning. There may be times when you'll feel like this again—when everything gets to be too much and you feel like something is missing, or you go through a rough patch. But there will be so many times when you *won't* feel like this. Your life has potential, and the possibility contained in that fact will never go away.

We cannot predict the future, and therefore we have no way of telling how long we'll feel this way. But it's impossible to feel *one thing* forever! What we do know is that the future holds loads of different choices and situations for you to experience, and each will bring something different to your life. Maybe your life feels empty now, but at some point soon it will again fill up with one of these opportunities. This could be a new friend, a new job, a hobby you try out and find that you're actually really good at. It could even be a book or a film—anything that inspires you. You will be filled with hope, love, and excitement again. For now, unfortunately, you'll have to ride out this uncomfortable feeling. You don't have to push yourself to try and feel positive things if you don't want to, though. It is okay to rest mentally, to let your mind just be for a little while.

You'll soon have the energy to get back up and try to let new feelings in again. But for now, all you gotta do is rest and be kind to yourself. Just because you may not be doing something "meaningful" right now doesn't mean you won't create something meaningful in the future. Right now, you're learning how to get through hard times and you're growing in strength every day. Dealing with this feeling is something you'll take into the future. The next time you feel this way you'll remember that last time, you made it through.

If you want to start feeling more attached to yourself, here are some things you can do:

- Put on some of your favorite songs. If you have ones that you just love to dance to, those are the ones! They might spark good memories of when you last heard them and enjoyed listening to them!
- Sit in the sun and let your skin soak in the heat. This physical sensation can sometimes help with grounding and prevent dissociation. An alternative to this could be running your hand under cold water for a minute or so.
- Find some objects that have a strong texture and run your fingers across the texture as many times as you want. Again, this helps with grounding. You could even take your shoes and socks off (if you're in a safe

environment) and feel different textures on your feet.

- Look at some old photos, as they may help trigger good memories, too.

## WORRY BOX: ASKING FOR A FRIEND

"A close friend of mine has struggled with depression for years now, but he's going through a particularly rough patch at the moment. I'm trying to be supportive and understand what he's feeling, but somehow I never seem to be able to make him feel any better. I see so much information on the internet about 'what not to say' or 'what not to do,' but I'm struggling to find any tips on what the right thing is. Could you help me out? All I want is to try and make even the tiniest difference, and be a good friend."

Hi there! The fact that you're taking the time to reach out and look for information on how to help your friend is really lovely. Please do note that the experience is different for everyone, so these suggestions might not be relevant. However, there's no harm in asking your friend what he needs or what would help him. I've asked people in the mental health community that I oversee what things help them when they're struggling, and the answers were things like people saying, "I am here to listen," "You can reach out to me," and, "You are doing better than you think."

It's good to remind them that they are loved and cared for, and that people want to listen to how they're feeling. It's easy to feel isolated and as if no one understands, and that's why it's important to show up for them. Make sure that they know you're there, even if they're not sure what they need yet. There's no easy fix when it comes to mental health, so just calmly being there for them long-term is often the best thing you can do. If things are seemingly quite bad for them, it may be a good idea for you to help them get professional support if you think they may need it. You can do this by looking into how to get mental health treatment in your area (often by going to a general practitioner). Thank you for being a kind and caring person.

## WORRY BOX: GOING BACK TO WORK

"I had a burnout a few years back and I've been unable to work since. I became severely depressed, and now that I am getting better I am absolutely terrified of going back to a workplace. So much so that I can't even mention it to my amazing therapist. I fear it will kill me. I'm thinking of doing something completely different than I used to, but I don't know what. Do you have any advice?"

Going back to work after taking time off for an illness is really daunting. You're not wrong to feel worried about it. First of all, give yourself some credit for coming so far in recovery that you're even considering going back to work. That's incredible, and it must have taken a lot of strength.

It's okay to be scared, but just mentioning the idea to your therapist (or to anyone) doesn't mean you have to do it straight away. You can talk about it, take more time to work out if you're ready, and ponder what the steps may be in preparing to do so. Take it at your own pace, without putting pressure on yourself to go back if you decide you're not quite ready. With your therapist, you can make a plan that incorporates finding something different to do than your previous job. A therapist is not just there to treat your depression; they are there to help you to work out how to deal with it in the real world, especially in everyday situations such as work. They are aware that it's not an easy thing for you to do and will support you in it.

## WORRY BOX: WHEN THINGS ARE GETTING BETTER

> "I have struggled with depression for several years now, with the last year being my lowest point in particular, including some attempts to end my life. Things are better but still not really great, even though I'm not where I was last year. Everyone thinks I'm 'better,' particularly my mom, who I feel doesn't truly understand what happened to me over the last eight years."

Your battle is valid. Depression is really, really hard to deal with, and it can be very frustrating when someone you love doesn't understand your struggle or think that it's valid. It's important to remember that no matter the opinions of others, everything you've gone through is important. Your feelings are important.

You are so brave for battling depression for so long and you should be proud of your progress in the process. You've come so far to be able to feel improvement in yourself. It's hard to open up sometimes, but having a conversation with your mom about your struggle may help her understand how things have been for you. Things feel obvious to us when we feel them so strongly, but people don't always see it from the outside, and they may not understand the extent of our struggle. It's okay to open up about this and about how depression has affected your life.

## WORRY BOX: AM I REALLY OKAY?

"I have depression and anxiety. I am taking meds
for both. I have made huge improvements. But I
worry that it's a lie. I worry that I'm pretending to
feel better. I don't trust that it's okay to feel okay. I
worry that I'm not really okay."

Making improvements is great! However, adjusting
to the new routine of life that comes with those
improvements can be scary. It's no surprise that
you're overthinking how you're feeling. Being able
to trust what *you* know, rather than what anxiety
and overthinking are saying, is key here. It sounds
to me like your anxiety is trying to override your
recovery. It's making you doubt yourself and pick
out every detail that could mean you're not okay.
Anxiety isn't correct, it's irrational, and that
means what it's saying isn't true. Put your trust
in the fact that you've made huge improvements,
because you have. You're doing great—tell anxiety
that it's wrong.

# WORRY BOX: UPSETTING DIAGNOSES

"I just got diagnosed with clinical depression.
My psychiatrist wants to monitor me for BD,
OCD, or GAD just in case. My mom went with me
to the consultation and was interviewed by the
psychiatrist, and I have no idea what they talked
about, but she hasn't stopped crying since. I don't
know if she's mad, scared, or feels like she's a bad
parent, but it makes me feel so guilty. That, because
of my disorder, I hurt my mom. I know it isn't really
my fault, but I still feel like it is."

To the person who submitted this: it is NOT your
fault. I know you feel guilty because your mom is
upset, but that doesn't mean you *made* her upset.
She loves you and doesn't want you to be going
through this; you can't be responsible for what
she's feeling. It'll take a while for her to adjust—it's
really scary finding out that your child has any
kind of illness. But again, this is not your fault.
You can't help the fact that you're struggling. It's
definitely much better that you have a diagnosis,
so both the doctor and your mom can help you
to get better. It might be hard to see now, but
it's better that your mom is involved, too. Now

she's aware of what's going on and can help and support you. This will take a while to process, but eventually, you'll both be at peace with your mental health struggle *and* your journey to seek treatment! Good luck.

# PART 5

# SOMETIMES YOU CAN'T SEE YOUR OWN LIGHT

# DON'T FORGET TO KEEP SOME LOVE FOR YOURSELF

## CHAPTER 17

# When You're Struggling to Find Self-Confidence

Confidence can often feel like an all-or-nothing deal, but it doesn't necessarily have to be that way. Of course, loving all of yourself and believing in everything you do is ideal, but for some people, achieving that can feel impossible. You might be thinking, "There's no way on earth that I'm ever going to have self-confidence," or, "I just feel like I fail at everything." Believe me, you're not the only one. However, there are ways you can start to break down these thoughts and tackle confidence straight on.

**First:** forget the idea that self-confidence is all-or-nothing. You don't need to feel good about yourself every moment of the day to have confidence in yourself. It may seem like some people do actually have that, but I assure you that's not the case. Think of someone that you believe to have self-love just oozing out of them—it could be someone you know in real life, at work or school, or even someone on social media. I'm here to tell you that they, too, have days where they don't feel confident. They're only human, and they can't feel great every day.

Feeling good about yourself doesn't have to be one giant accomplishment. You can break it down into little victories, all of which can be done one at a time to try and help you feel happier with yourself. You can feel confident about one thing about yourself, but not so great about others, and that's still super amazing! How about this: every week, write down three things you like about yourself. Try it like this:

1. One thing you like about your personality.

2. One thing you like about your life/what you do.

3. One thing you like about your physical appearance.

An example could be:

1. My kindness toward other people.

2. When I write.

3. My curly hair.

## COMPLIMENTING YOURSELF

Write down three things you like about yourself each week to remember to be kind to YOU!

### ONE THING YOU LIKE ABOUT YOUR...

...PERSONALITY:

♥

...LIFE/WHAT YOU DO:

♥

...PHYSICAL APPEARANCE:

♥

### ONE THING YOU LIKE ABOUT YOUR...

...PERSONALITY:

♥

...LIFE/WHAT YOU DO:

♥

...PHYSICAL APPEARANCE:

♥

### ONE THING YOU LIKE ABOUT YOUR...

...PERSONALITY:

♥

...LIFE/WHAT YOU DO:

♥

...PHYSICAL APPEARANCE:

♥

Try to choose things that make you smile, even if just a little bit. If you're struggling with this, please remember that you deserve self-love. It's easier said than done, I know, but it's true. Your confidence might be blocked by feeling unworthy of liking yourself, as if what you are and what you have are not enough. But it is. This leads me to my next point.

To practice gaining self-confidence, **my second point is:** remember that you don't have to change yourself to like yourself. When you reflect on everything about yourself, stop pointing out all the things you want to change. Instead, point out all the things that are so brilliant, they don't need changing (which is most of you!). Comparing yourself to someone else's body, work, or assets will never allow you to be happy with what *you've* got.

There's someone out there looking at you and thinking the same thing—comparing themselves to you and what you have. We all spend so much time focusing on other people and trying to figure out how to change ourselves to be more like them that we completely lose sight of the fact that what we have is enough. Your skills, your dreams, your hair, your clothes, your body—they are all enough because they are yours. They are what make you, and you are absolutely worthy, valid, and deserving just the way you are. You don't need someone else's *this* or some else's *that* to be good or beautiful. You already are.

**My third point is this:** forget the idea that you're not allowed to have self-confidence after you've made a mistake. We all make mistakes from time to time. We all learn from them and grow as people. You don't deserve to be punished with self-hate just because you made a mistake. Spending your time filling your body up with frustration isn't helpful. Kicking yourself every time you think about the mistake isn't helpful either.

Anger over getting something wrong turns into self-hate. We use these mistakes to build up a list of reasons for why we think we don't deserve something, or why we don't believe in ourselves. Right now, you're probably holding onto so many little mistakes, downfalls, and difficulties that are stopping you from feeling better about yourself. This is such a destructive way of thinking. That negativity will hold you down. Instead, grab onto those things and tell them you forgive them. Forgive *yourself*. Then let them go. Practice the process of self-forgiveness for every negative thing you weaponize as an excuse for not liking yourself. By doing this, you'll make space to let the positivity in. Space to understand that, despite mistakes, you still deserve to feel good about yourself.

**My fourth and final point is:** delete the idea that self-confidence makes you a selfish or arrogant person. It doesn't. All that happens when your self-confidence grows, other than you feeling happier about yourself, is that your life becomes easier. That can never be a bad thing. When you're not bombarded by voices of self-hate, you get through the day feeling stronger.

We're often presented with the idea that if someone is showing how much they love themselves, they must be "full of it," "self-absorbed," or "arrogant." The thing is, believing in yourself is not *any of those things.* It's giving yourself enough importance to know what you deserve, how capable you are, and how much you can shine. This can be on a big scale or a minor scale—you can shine at wearing clothes that make you feel good, or you can shine at completing a project. You don't have to feel like you're shining when you're sitting at home watching TV though, because remember, you're only human!

Something I love to do is stick some Post-it Notes around my mirror with encouraging phrases on them. Most of the time, before we start the day, we look in the mirror. Isn't it great to have some small reminders there to offer a quick boost in positivity? You can create your own by cutting up some squares of paper with tape or using sticky notes (if you have some), and writing things that you need to be reminded of that make you feel empowered.

You can also look online for some ideas, if you'd like. If you can't think of any right now, you can always keep adding to the mirror as you find things that make you feel inspired. Here are some you can use.

YOU
MATTER
SO
MUCH ♥

YOU
ARE
STRONG
♡ ♡ ♡

YOU'RE
GREAT!

YOU
ARE
NEEDED

TAKE
CARE
OF
YOURSELF

YOU ARE
LOVED

CUT THESE OUT

YOU
MATTER
SO
MUCH ♥

YOU
ARE
STRONG
♡  ♡  ♡

YOU'RE
GREAT!

YOU
ARE
NEEDED

TAKE
CARE
OF
YOURSELF

YOU ARE
LOVED

## CHAPTER 18

# When You Can't See Your Capabilities

Remember that time you thought you couldn't do something and you did? You can do it again.

Sometimes we get stuck in a negative thought loop of self-doubt. That negative voice kicks in and we can't see our own capabilities, even if we've done those things before. When you're feeling doubtful of yourself, reflect on previous times you've felt this way and proven yourself wrong. Remember all the times you did something you thought you couldn't do? It's happened more than you think. We tend to give more weight to the voice of self-doubt than to the fact that we actually did it!

The truth is, you do so many little things each day that, in the long run, add up! It's all about perspective. You don't give yourself credit for the things you *are* doing because you either don't think they are enough, or you've become so used to your routine that you can't see how much you've accomplished. You are more capable than you know. You do things all the time without even giving yourself credit. Look at how many things you've done this week; have you stopped even once to compliment yourself, or encourage yourself to keep going? If not, why not try it now?

For a few minutes, just sit and give yourself a compliment. If you feel a little silly doing it or cringe at your own words, push through the cringe. Say it out loud. Think of something, anything, that you've done this week. Now say, "I am so proud of myself for doing that." You can replace the compliment with anything you'd like, but make sure you're pointing out something you accomplished today or this week.

Wanna know what else is true? You did that thing, despite every obstacle that life threw at you this week—emotions, exhaustion, relationship drama, feeling under the weather, lack of motivation, lack of self-confidence. You still got up and you did it, and that's so great!

Now that we've taken the time to really understand that we do more than we think, let's focus on one of the reasons you may have picked up this book. Is it because you want to be able to do things with confidence, but feel like you're unable? If so, follow this flow chart.

# CONFIDENCE FLOW CHART

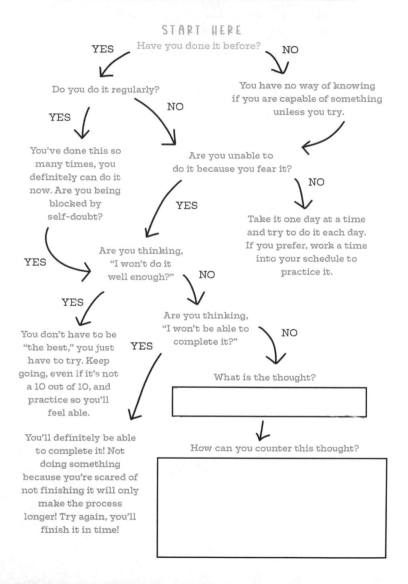

START HERE
Have you done it before?

YES

NO

Do you do it regularly?

You have no way of knowing
if you are capable of something
unless you try.

YES

NO

You've done this so
many times, you
definitely can do it
now. Are you being
blocked by
self-doubt?

Are you unable to
do it because you fear it?

NO

YES

Take it one day at a time
and try to do it each day.
If you prefer, work a time
into your schedule to
practice it.

YES

Are you thinking,
"I won't do it
well enough?"

NO

YES

You don't have to be
"the best," you just
have to try. Keep
going, even if it's not
a 10 out of 10, and
practice so you'll
feel able.

YES

Are you thinking,
"I won't be able to
complete it?"

NO

What is the thought?

YES

You'll definitely be able
to complete it! Not
doing something
because you're scared of
not finishing it will only
make the process
longer! Try again, you'll
finish it in time!

How can you counter this thought?

Let's make sure we are talking to ourselves with positive words rather than negative ones.

- Instead of saying, "I can't do this," say, "I can do this."

- Instead of saying, "I'm never going to be able to do it," say, "I will get there with practice."

- Instead of saying, "I'm stupid for finding this hard," say, "It's okay to find something difficult, I will take my time to complete it."

# NEGATIVE VS. POSITIVE TALK

Replace the negative words you say to yourself
with positive ones.

| NEGATIVE | POSITIVE |
|---|---|
|  |  |

## CHAPTER 19

# When You're Feeling Insecure

We often feel insecure when we hold ourselves to unrealistic standards. The feeling of not being good enough comes from this idea that we need to be something *more* than what we are. Self-judgement takes over and tells us what we "should" or "shouldn't" be like—but things are never that clean cut. There is no right way you need to be. There is no right or wrong way to be *yourself*.

Insecurity sometimes stems from feeling like you don't know "who you are." As I'm sure you're aware, this is one of the big questions in life that we all consider. Getting to know yourself and choosing how to define yourself can be a confusing process. I talked to my friend Margherita Barbieri about this, as she talks often about self-love and eating disorder recovery (@alwaysmargi on Instagram, if you want to check her out!). I explained to her my belief that who we are can be fluid, depending on the things that make us happy. She asked me what I meant by that, and I'm gonna try to explain the way I see it:

What makes you who you are isn't *just* one thing, it's *many* things. You're kind of like your own solar system. Imagine that, within yourself, you have loads of stars, and each one of those stars is something that makes you who you are. They could be anything: activities you enjoy and are passionate about, your emotions and feelings, your beliefs and values, your dreams, or your favorite things. As we grow, who we are can change (meaning that the process is fluid) because some of those stars may shine brighter on some days than others. You see, we don't enjoy the same things to the same degree every single day. These things change throughout our life. You may feel happy doing something one year, and in a few years you grow out of it. You can always find a new thing to love, enjoy, or believe in. These add new stars, new parts of the solar system that makes you!

As you grow, you'll go through stages where new stars replace ones that aren't as important to you anymore. That's okay. We're not going to be made of the same constellations our whole lives—kind of like the night sky, just on fast forward. It's fine to not know who you are right now; you're likely transforming and creating new constellations inside of you. You won't feel lost forever. You shine so bright, even if you can't see it yourself...but one day you will.

**Stars are constantly being born and dying in the skies above us. The sky isn't any less beautiful just because it's lit in different places. It will take us a little while to adjust our telescopes to see and appreciate the new ones within ourselves.**

Write a letter of forgiveness to yourself. You can write it entirely from scratch, or you can fill in the blanks of this sample one I wrote for you. Through this exercise, you can practice letting in self-love by forgiving yourself for feeling insecure.

## SELF-FORGIVENESS LETTER

Fill in the blanks with words that are relevant to you.

Dear _____

I forgive you for _____.
I am sorry I have called you mean things; you are
not _____ or _____. You are _____
and _____. I forgive you for all the things
you have done "wrong," because self-hate will not
help you move forward and you do not deserve it.
You are allowed to make mistakes. I am sorry for
getting _____ at you sometimes, I know
you are really trying. It's okay if you find things
_____ a lot of the time, but this does not make
you _____. You are strong and _____
and if you forgive me, we can fight these difficult
feelings together. Thank you for _____

_____

_____

_____

_____

_____, and
keep going!
From _____

## WORRY BOX: NOT FEELING "ENOUGH"

"I feel as though I will never amount to anything and that I'm not good enough for anyone, whether that be friendships or relationships. I have been cheated on twice before, and I also have an ex-boyfriend who gave up on the relationship because he moved away. Now I keep trying to get to know people but it never works out, and I feel like I'm not good enough. As for friends, no matter how good I am to them or how much I'm there for them, they never seem to care about me properly, and there's always someone else they'd rather talk to or be with. So I guess I just keep asking myself...am I not enough?"

You don't need approval from someone else to feel like you're enough. I know that's difficult to believe, but it's true. The actions of the people who have left you before are not an indication of your worth. Whether they stayed or not doesn't change the fact that you *are* enough. Sometimes it takes a while to find people we click with; not everyone loves everyone all of the time, and that's okay. It might seem like they don't care about you because you're struggling to absorb love. You might be closed off to the idea because you don't feel like you deserve it, but you do. It's okay to search and continue to try and make new friends until you find someone who values you, who treats you with care and supports you in what you're going through. Friends are supposed to help you up, not pull you down, remember that!

## WORRY BOX: NEGATIVE SELF-BELIEF

"I feel like I'm not good at anything. Everyone else looks like they are really skilled and I'm always average at or bad at everything I do."

I think you're being too hard on yourself! If you're harboring this much self-doubt, it's likely that you're better at what you're doing than you realize. Something to remember is that you don't have to be the *best* at something in order to be *good* at it. You also don't have to do it perfectly for it to still be fun and good. You have skills, and you can do it! Rather than spending time comparing what you can do to what other people are doing, compare what you're doing to what *you* have done before. The way to build skills is to improve your own, not observe those of other people. With that said, it's also important that you just enjoy it, too!

## PART 6

# IT'S OKAY TO JUST NEED REST

## CHAPTER 20

# When Anxiety Strikes in the Middle of the Night

When you're trying to sleep but can't because you're experiencing anxious thoughts, I'm sure you (like most people) attempt to control those thoughts. Do you try to replace your worries with literally anything else, in an effort to decrease your anxiety? This is actually keeping you awake longer.

Not only does this make your mind work harder, and therefore keep you awake, but it also isn't really effective. Your brain is an organ just like your heart, lungs, and kidneys. If you were to try and tell your heart to stop beating, would it? No. This works similarly with your brain—it will still think what it wants, whether you tell it to or not.

I know the urge to distract your mind in this way is strong, and that you really want to stop feeling anxious, but force isn't the answer. What will help is—I know this will sound crazy!—letting those thoughts pass through. However, as you do this, reassure yourself that everything is okay, because it is.

These anxious thoughts can't hurt you because they aren't true. They're only worries, and have no element of fact to them. You can and should let these concerns pass on their own. Rather than trying to control the thoughts causing your anxiety, try to alleviate your anxious feelings by grounding yourself. Try to calm yourself with reminders that, no matter what the thoughts say, you are still just as okay as you were before they were there! This way, even if you have bubbling worries, you're able to remain calm. I'm aware that this is a lot easier said than done, and it will take a lot of practice, but it is worth it!

## HEALTH ANXIETY AND SLEEP

If you have health anxiety, you know how common it is for it to come knocking at your door at 1:00 a.m. when you're trying to sleep. It can be the scariest experience, having your mind try to convince you that something bad is happening to your body. I know it's so hard to control. If you're experiencing this now, I'm here to remind you that you are safe. No matter what your mind says, you are safe, and your body is okay. Believe me, your body knows how to look after itself.

The first thing you'll likely want to do is to seek reassurance from loved ones. This can be a little difficult if it's happening in the middle of the night. The good news is, that obstacle is actually helpful. As hard as it may be, I recommend trying to *not* ask for reassurance from other people. It may sound like a silly suggestion, but every time you ask for reassurance, it makes it harder for you to trust *your own* judgement. Anxiety tends to make you feel like you can't believe your own word, or that reassurance from someone else is more accurate. This is not true. You *can* trust your own judgement and understand that you are okay (even if you don't completely feel that way yet). Doing this can be really difficult, but it does help.

I learned this tip when my therapist and I mapped out the things that were fueling my health anxiety. Every time my health anxiety started to creep in, especially when I was trying to sleep, the first thing I wanted to do was wake someone up and tell them about all the dangerous physical symptoms I was convinced I was having. I needed them to listen and tell me that I was fine, that the physical sensations I was feeling were normal, not dangerous, and that it was in fact just my anxiety. I learned that this fuels the cycle of anxiety and does not do me any favors.

The cycle of anxiety tends to go like this:

# THE HEALTH ANXIETY CYCLE

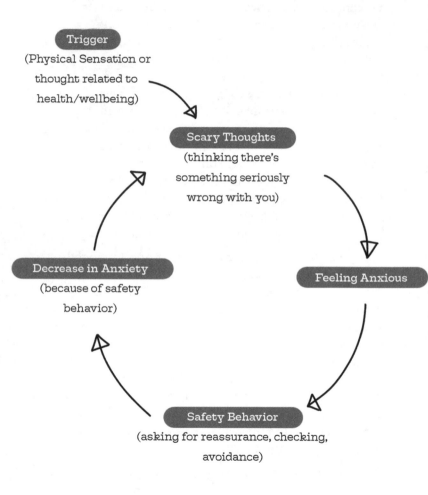

Trigger
(Physical Sensation or thought related to health/wellbeing)

Scary Thoughts
(thinking there's something seriously wrong with you)

Feeling Anxious

Safety Behavior
(asking for reassurance, checking, avoidance)

Decrease in Anxiety
(because of safety behavior)

After learning this, I realized that I needed to break the cycle and finally stop my habitual time-consuming health anxiety from taking over my entire night's sleep. To break this cycle, you need to be able to tell yourself that you're safe when a trigger comes, and you need to truly believe it. That way you're reassuring yourself as the anxiety increases, or even before it starts. If you're finding this too difficult and can't find the words to reassure yourself, then the one and only thing you need to do is try your best to stop yourself from doing any other safety behaviors (responses to health anxiety) while you're trying to fall asleep. These can include:

- ◉ Checking your body for symptoms while you're trying to sleep (feeling parts of your body, moving around to check parts of your body, testing how you're breathing, feeling your pulse/heartbeat, etc.)
- ◉ Mentally checking your body
- ◉ Asking for reassurance from someone else
- ◉ Googling symptoms

These things may give you some temporary relief, but they will not help long-term. If you can cut that cycle at step one, "Trigger," you're likelier to get more sleep. I don't know about you, but when health anxiety is out of control, the feeling of doom can last all night. We want to stop that from happening! Instead of doing something that's going to continue that cycle, think of some things that can help blast a giant hole through it. To do this, I recommend trying these things:

- Practice setting a worry time. You can read about this in part 2, chapter 6.
- Shift your focus onto something else. As soon as you start to feel anxious, find a healthy distraction. This helps orient your mind away from the physical sensations. Some healthy distractions include reading, watching something, or doing a word search or puzzle. More healthy distractions are listed in chapter 5.

## AFFIRMATIONS FOR REASSURANCE

I have felt this way before and I was safe then. I am safe now.
I know that bodily sensations are simply heightened when I am anxious. Everything is okay.
I remember that symptoms of anxiety sometimes include chest pains. My body is recovering.
I do not have to let anxiety control me. I can say, "No, you are wrong. I am safe."

## CHAPTER 21

# When You Can't Sleep Because Your Brain's Too Awake

There are some steps you can take to prevent this sort of thing from happening. You may have heard these before in, but in case you haven't, here are some helpful tips:

- ⊙ **Stop working a few hours before you go to bed.** If you're a busy person and you work long nights, that can likely cause an inability to wind down. When you work very late, you don't give your brain time to transition into a more relaxed mode. Your body doesn't want to sleep when it's in work mode. It's really important to have time between working and sleeping to allow yourself time to unwind. Leave your stressed, fast-working brain power in work mode, and chill into the evening with sleep mode. Many people do this by watching a movie or TV show before they go to bed. This helps refocus their mind away from work! If TV isn't your thing, you can read a book, spend time with a loved one, or listen to some music.

Anything non-work-related that uses a lower level of concentration is good to do before bed!

⊙ **Implement a nighttime routine.** This could include going to bed at the same time every day, not eating too late, making time to wind down before you go to bed, and making sure you've done everything you need to before getting ready for bed. Some people like to incorporate nighttime yoga or meditation into their routine, too. If trouble sleeping is a regular problem, it's worth making an evening routine. Even if it doesn't work right away, you will eventually experience the calming benefits it provides.

⊙ **Get everything ready for the next day before you go to bed.** If you're leaving the house the next day, pack your bag, plan what you're going to wear, and plan what you're going to take for lunch. It's important to take as many things off your mind as you can. It's important to take as many things off your mind as you can, and getting everything ready beforehand helps to do that.

The thing that's helped me with my inability to sleep at proper times has been keeping my mind occupied just before I go to sleep. I find that if I focus too much on trying to sleep, I overthink about the potential reasons *why* I can't sleep.

If you can't sleep because you're worried, try drawing a worry tree (something my therapist suggested to me). You do this with pen and paper, or by using worry tree apps. It might sound strange to advise someone to get up and do an activity when all they want to do is sleep, but sometimes getting up and doing something for a while can help redirect your body into sleep mode.

Follow the questions in the worry tree diagram to help you process your worries. You can do this with as many worries as you like. This should help empty the things you're thinking about onto the page, so you won't have them circling around in your mind anymore. Sometimes worries just need to be listened to and acknowledged; in doing so, you realize that they're irrational and you can't do anything about them. This process of listing ideas isn't one that everyone finds helpful, but even if you do it and don't stop worrying right away, it may still help you sleep.

# CREATING A WORRY TREE

Notice the worry

↓

Ask yourself: What am I worrying about?

↓

Ask yourself: Can I do something about this?

Yes

No

Make a plan of action

Let the worry go

↓

Can you do it now?

Yes

No

Do it

Schedule it

Let the worry go

Focus your attention on something else.

(Because you can't do anything about it, this worry doesn't need your attention!)

The main message I want to impart to you is this: if you can't sleep right now, don't panic. This night will eventually end and tomorrow will come. It can be frustrating to be so tired and feel like you're unable to do anything about it, but I promise you, it's okay. You'll eventually catch up on the sleep you're missing and feel better. It's easy to get annoyed at your exhaustion, but try to remember that it isn't your fault. Sleep just kind of does its own thing; you can't control it, so try not to force it. Lying there and jamming your eyes shut probably won't make slumber more likely. Your body will do so when it's ready, so try your best to calm down. The night won't last forever, even if it feels like you've been laying on the pillow for an eternity. It really is going to be okay.

Below are some words from my friend Dan Carver about her experience with sleeping difficulties:

> I've never had a good relationship with sleep for as long as I can remember. I've spent countless nights staring at the wall or the ceiling for hours, only to have to wake up after four hours. A lot of times, I give up before I even try to fall asleep. I'll talk with people until 1 a.m., or work into the night because I know I would have gone to bed at that time anyway.

Being tired doesn't change anything either. I can be exhausted already, running on a few hours of sleep, get into bed, and still not be able to fall asleep for another hour or so. People suggest things like reading, going to bed earlier, getting off of technology an hour before bed, etc.—and for a 'normal' person with functional mental health, that's probably great advice, but none of it ever really works for me (although I know it all comes from a place of love and concern).

Recently, I've been writing a bit of a diary before I go to bed. I just get all my anxieties and worries of the day out of my brain. It's never really coherent or neat, but it's always so helpful to just collect everything in one place that isn't my head. Venting out my problems has stopped them from nagging at me so much, and I can come back to them later to try and understand how I can make changes that will positively affect my mental health, like having a routine and keeping up-to-date with friends. It's not always about finding a solution for the problem, but finding a healthy coping mechanism for it in the meantime.

## CHAPTER 22

# When You Haven't Slept and Have to Function All Day Long

If you've had no sleep, the last thing you want to do is get up and do your normal business, but sometimes you just have to. You'd be surprised at how much of an impact sleep has on your mental state. If you tend to feel super emotional after not sleeping well, then you're not alone! I totally get you. When we don't sleep, our brains are exhausted—both from spending the entire night worrying about being unable to sleep, and from going through the full day you had before that. Having to then pile more things onto your plate doesn't usually work out very well. I hear you: you're absolutely, flat-out exhausted and all you want to do is sleep. Know that, no matter how much your emotions are overwhelming you, you can handle them. You can take the day off and rest. If that's what you need to do today, please don't feel guilty for that. It's not your fault you couldn't sleep. If resting is what's best for you and you're in a situation where you can do that, then do it. That being said, if you have commitments today and you have to do them, then you don't have much of a choice. But that doesn't mean you have to be hard on yourself. Be gentle. Find a kind voice and speak to yourself calmly throughout the day. Give yourself helpful encouragement.

I cannot stress this enough: even if you're not hungry, please eat and drink water regularly. Exhaustion can make you lose your appetite. Being anxious about doing a day's work and running on no sleep can make you lose your appetite. Having a stressful day can make you lose your appetite. Food and sleep are your only sources of energy, so you can't cancel them both out—that's self-sabotage. Food is fuel, and it's important that you fuel up your body. Also, when it comes to routine, even if you wake up tired, get dressed as you usually would. This will help you stick to the normality of your routine and help make your day feel less up in the air. Don't forget that the day will come to an end and you'll be able to sleep again. You just have to find the strength to handle the stress today, for a few hours. And you can do it. If you can, please take breaks any and every time they're offered to you (and in those breaks, be sure to eat and drink). If given the opportunity, talk to people. Their social energy can help you stay awake, too, no matter how zombie-like your body currently feels.

This day is only one day, and you are bigger than this day. You'll get through this day. If you're feeling like you can't do it, your mind may be getting overwhelmed. When you're tired, your capacity to do things often decreases because you've not had a break from thinking. If this is happening, please revert back to taking things one at a time. Take the task at hand first, and only once you've completed it should you take on the next thing. You're absolutely amazing for even trying to get through this day, so if things are getting to be too much, take it easy. Don't beat yourself up for finding it hard!

## WORRY BOX: HEALTH ANXIETY

"People call me a baby. They say I'm being stupid and overreacting. But I can't help worrying about everything. I don't understand how my mind works. A headache turns into an imagined brain tumor and I stress about the littlest thing. I don't believe doctors when they diagnose me, and every ache or pain has me focusing on worrying about it. I can't keep this up. I can't keep worrying—it's exhausting. I just want it to end."

I can't tell you how much I relate to your submission. It sounds to me like you're struggling with some symptoms of health anxiety (hypochondria), a type of anxiety disorder where you obsessively worry about your health and well-being. It causes you to think that every ache or pain is something that's really wrong with you. I know these anxious feelings you're experiencing are so, so exhausting, but you can get help to address them. Having anxiety doesn't make you pathetic, nor does it mean you're overreacting. Your brain thinks a certain way and makes you feel really scared. Your reaction is a result of the intense thoughts and feelings you're experiencing.

It doesn't make you stupid. Anxiety can feel like an endless cycle, but you *can* get better. I highly advise that you reach out and try to get mental health support. You can do this by seeing a doctor. You don't deserve to live with this much fear. You deserve support for the way your mind is affecting you.

## WORRY BOX: AN OVERWORKING MIND

"I feel anxious and tired all the time, even when I'm sleeping. Each day feels exhausting."

It sounds like your mind's in overdrive. It's astonishing how much of an effect our mental health can have on our physical health. You can sit still all day, doing nothing strenuous at all, and still feel exhausted from the circles your thoughts keep making in your head. Anxiety takes up so much energy, it's no wonder you feel tired. During the day, make sure you set some time aside to do something that'll give your mind a rest from thinking. I often read or watch a show, because it makes my thoughts connect to a character in the story rather than to myself for a little while. Little chunks of time to slow your mind will help.

# PART 7

# YOU DESERVE HAPPINESS

EXCUSE ME?
CAN WE
PAUSE FOR A
SECOND TO
CELEBRATE YOU?

CHAPTER 23

# When You're Feeling Excited about the Future

The fact that you've flipped to this page is the best news ever. Congratulations on your excitement!

Even though you're feeling excited about the future, it's important to make sure that you're planning realistically to keep this momentum going. Be mindful and take into account how your everyday mood can fluctuate. It can be difficult to envision the future you want when you're struggling with your mental health, and the negative days often outweigh the positive. However, that doesn't mean the scales won't soon turn the other way! It also doesn't mean that you shouldn't feel excited or make plans for the future. When making these plans, just make sure you're not holding yourself to impractical standards. There's a difference between planning for your future and pressuring yourself into it! You cannot expect to feel positive every day, and that's okay— no one does!

When you're feeling this excited—especially if you don't experience this feeling often—it's good to write a list of the things you're hopeful for. It's completely fine if the things on the list aren't huge life goals! Little things are just as important. We do more little things in our lives than big things, and so the small and fun activities we do could even be more important than the big ones. Aim for small wins. These can be any number of things: planning to attend a day trip or event with a friend, taking a yoga class, planning an upcoming vacation, creating something like artwork or music, or writing. Whatever you're looking forward to in your future, write it down!

## THINGS I AM HOPEFUL FOR

♥

♥

♥

♥

♥

♥

♥

♥

♥

♥

♥

♥

♥

♥

♥

♥

♥

If you also want to focus on big things, you can do this visualization exercise. When you're feeling excited about the future, close your eyes and picture the scenario in your head. Ask yourself:

- When you think of your future, what do you *see*?

- How does it *feel* when you imagine it?

- What's making you excited about it?

- Try and visualize everything about it—the location, the people, maybe even a new job. What's surrounding you?

- Is there a specific moment you're thinking of? If so, is that a goal you have in mind for your future? If yes, are you doing anything right now to work toward it?

Once you've done this exercise, if you want to and don't think it'll put too much pressure on you, write down the things that need to happen for you to *arrive* at that future you're looking toward. Remember, this task is meant to reduce the stress of planning for your future, NOT add to it. Some people find planning really useful, whereas others don't. It's completely up to you. Look at the diagram on the next page.

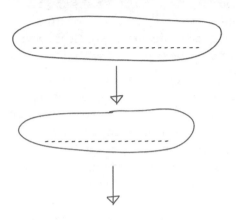

Start by filling out the first bubble at the top of the page with the thing you just imagined. If it's too big or there are too many things to fit into that space, just pick one for now and roll with it.

Now, move down to the next one, working backwards in the order of things you need to do. For example, say you want to buy a house. You can't go straight from having no house to just buying one. You need to go house hunting to find the right one. But before that, you need to decide on the area in which you want to live. And before *that*, you need to either sell the house you currently live in or give notice that you're leaving a rented property. And even before that, you need to save money to buy the house.

It's likely you can't go straight to your end goal either, so put some steps in place that'll help you get there! When doing this, keep in mind that you have time—no one is expecting you to reach your end goal immediately. It's okay to take this one step at a time. Often for big goals, even getting to step one can be difficult. You're not a failure for finding it hard to take that first step.

If you're struggling with feeling excited about the future, here are some reminders:

- ◉ Good things are coming! You never know what's around the corner. Next week, you could get some good news, meet someone new, or be inspired by something. There are always good days in store for your future.

- There's an endless amount of possible experiences for you to live through! There are so many things you've not done yet—new things for you to try out, or old things you might revisit.
- You may not have even experienced the best day of your life yet! You never know what might top your current "favorite day." If nothing else, feel excited for the joy you'll reminisce on from that day.
- You're always growing. You never know: in the future, feeling excited may happen more often.

## CHAPTER 24

# When You're Having a Really Good Day

I am so happy you're having a good day! I know you must be thinking, "If I'm happy, then why do I need to read this part of the book?" Well this part—the "hopeful" part—is about making sure we note down and remember these feelings, so we can come back to them when our days aren't so great!

Every day you feel great, write down a journal entry about what you did that day. On days that feel impossible to get through, it's so easy to forget that there are good days. For the times you feel hopeless, let's make reminders from when you felt hopeful. Like a little letter to yourself, you can simply write, "You know what, today was a really good day."

There's a space for you to try it out here. If you enjoy this activity and find it helpful, then you may want to invest in getting a long-term journal, so you have more space to fill out on your own time! When journaling, you might want to consider

writing down which parts of the day you enjoyed
and how they made you feel.

_____

_____

_____

_____

_____

_____

_____

_____

_____

_____

_____

_____

_____

_____

_____

_____

_____

_____

_____

_____

_____

You can also take note of someone or something you were grateful for that day. If it was a person, write down what they did and how they helped make your day so great. You may even want to thank that person and give back to them: make them a thank-you card, send them a quick text, or go old-school and write them a letter of appreciation.

It's important to show gratitude to the people in your life and let them know what helps you, what you enjoy, and how much you value them! We get so wrapped up in our own minds, problems, and lives that we sometimes forget to reach out to others. You never know, that person may have *wanted* to help you out by doing whatever they did for you. Wouldn't it be great to let them know that it did in fact help? You don't know if *they* might be having a bad day, week, or month, and need someone to reach out and check on them. When we're filled with goodness, it's important to spread that around to the people we love—but make sure to leave enough for yourself, too.

On good days, be proud of yourself and let that sink in! At some point, you may be tempted to compare your good days to your bad days. Try to avoid this. Having a good day doesn't mean you should pressure yourself to feel that way for the rest of your life.

On a good day, you'll likely feel like you're achieving more because you're in a much more positive headspace. Sometimes that's true—you may be more productive or feel more able to achieve things that are too hard on bad days. I can't stress this enough: that is completely okay. Don't feel like you've failed on your bad days just because you haven't done as much as you would on a good day. Don't use the happier days, when things feel easier, as weapons of self-deprecation on your bad ones. Comparing the two won't do you any good, not to mention it's completely unfair.

**On a good day, most people feel:**

- Positive
- Productive
- Happier
- Less anxious/low
- Clear-minded
- Hopeful

**On a bad day, most people feel:**

- Tired
- Overwhelmed
- Low/anxious
- Heavy-minded
- Self-conscious

You can't expect to be able to complete the same tasks or to find the same amount of energy and bravery on both of those kinds of days! It's okay to have bad days and it's okay to have good days—both are part of life.

Bad days and good days look different for everyone. In the following space, remind yourself of how you experience them. Fill in the blanks with whatever fits you. While you're doing this, remember to be proud of yourself on *all* the days, not just the ones you find easier.

## GOOD DAYS VS. BAD DAYS

### ON A GOOD DAY, I FEEL:

### ON A BAD DAY, I FEEL:

Make sure to have fun on your really good days, too! If you overcrowd your good days with work and productivity-oriented tasks, you risk overdoing it and exhausting yourself. A good day is the perfect opportunity to do something you enjoy, something you'd find more difficult on a bad day. You may find the benefits of doing something fun are better than those of being productive, because a fun activity reconnects you with the joy of life. This can even make the good day last longer! You deserve to feel happy, to have fun, and to relax.

## CHAPTER 25

# When You Feel Good about Yourself

Hallelujah, you're finally starting to see how amazing you are! Okay, I know—I won't jinx it. I will say that I'm so proud of you for accepting self-love, even if it's just a small amount! You deserve it, don't doubt that for a second.

At this moment, I encourage you to listen to yourself, your body, and your mind, and let this feeling sink in. Connect with the glow that's giving you that self-confidence. That glow is pride. That glow is beautiful. Feel the contentment and confidence inside of you, without feeling silly or self-centered. This feeling happens when you let go of all the opinions around you, and you feel happy without needing other people's judgement or approval. You've probably heard this before, but I'm going to remind you: being *you* is your superpower. It's so true! When we feel good about ourselves, we embrace the respect, love, and care we deserve.

Today, you should do something for *you*—something that you would usually do to cheer yourself up. This time, do it because you know you deserve it. Have an in-home spa day, or go to the actual spa! Do some skincare or any type of physical self-care you like! Go shopping and get yourself something—spend a little on yourself! Do some yoga or meditate to help you relax! Cook your favorite meal just because!

It can even be something you would normally think to do for someone else, but this time, you're doing it for yourself: telling yourself to have a break, taking yourself out to do something fun, or giving yourself compliments.

Write something kind to yourself for future days when you may need a pep talk. In the space on the next page, you can do it in whatever format you like: a letter, list, or quote. You can even get creative if that's your thing. Use colored pencils and decorate the page!

_____
_____
_____
_____
_____
_____
_____
_____
_____
_____
_____
_____
_____
_____
_____
_____
_____
_____
_____
_____
_____
_____
_____
_____

You might want to pay attention to what is making you feel good about yourself today. Is it something you did? Is it something you're wearing that gives you confidence? Is it someone you've spent time with? It's good to remember these things, so we can surround ourselves with what makes us feel good and the people who lift us up.

## WHEN YOU ENJOYED SOMETHING

Yay! You enjoyed something! I assume that, since you're reading this, you've recently struggled to enjoy the things you normally would and it was starting to upset you. Nonetheless, you've now done something that you enjoy, and hopefully that makes you feel relieved, excited, or even buoyant! That's so great.

I want to make sure you're not feeling guilty for enjoying something. A lot of the time, our happiness is shadowed by guilt. We're stifled by thoughts that say we haven't worked hard enough to have fun, or that we should've been doing something more important. I'm here to remind you and say that's not true. Having fun is something you deserve no matter what, and you don't have to feel bad for taking time out to do something you like.

Now that you've found something you enjoy, let's use a mind map to brainstorm some other things that you may like. Write down a thing you enjoyed today in the middle of the page, then draw a circle around it. Whatever ideas come to you when you think of that activity, branch them out from the middle. You can look at the example to see what I mean.

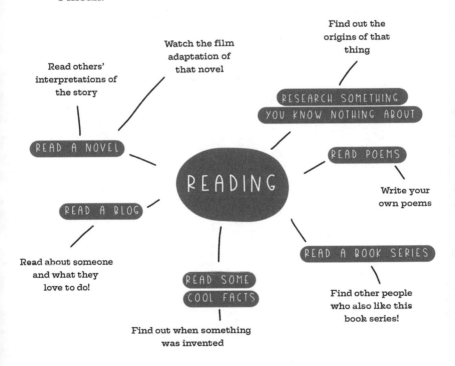

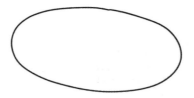

CHAPTER 26

# Sharing Some Happiness

This is usually where I'd share some worry box submissions from my website. However, as this emotion is positive and not worry-related, what I've chosen to do instead is share some happiness from strangers. I asked my followers and friends what their absolute favorite feelings in the world were, and this is what they said:

- The feeling of being creatively inspired. (That's mine!)
- Passion—being consumed by something that fuels and fires your soul.
- Being ninety feet below the surface of the ocean, hearing nothing but the bubbles of air escaping from my exhalations and feeling small in the vastness of the world. It's the most at peace and calm I've ever felt in my life.
- Achievement.
- The feeling of progress and growth, when you're finally able to do something you weren't

able to do before and you just feel like a magical being.

- The feeling of evolving and developing is consuming, in a beautiful way. You just feel like you could fly.
- Calmness.
- Contentment, either from the satisfaction of having achieved something or through being relaxed and genuinely enjoying life.
- The feeling when you get into bed and it's cold outside, so you bundle up in your blankets and duvet.
- Feeling happy to be alive.
- Being loved.
- Feeling adored.
- That moment when you realize, "Wow. This is so beautiful and I'm experiencing it."
- Laughing till you cry.
- The feeling when you're so excited about something that you could burst.
- Kissing my girlfriend.
- Feeling completely at home, like I belong—it's like a weight lifting off my shoulders.
- Waking up to warm, sunny Sunday mornings makes me smile and feel so happy.
- Being hugged by someone I love.
- That feeling when you come home and see your dog at the door.

- ◉ Sunshine on my face.
- ◉ Listening to waves.
- ◉ Eating something fantastic.
- ◉ The feeling of love...haha! That rich, warming, gooey feeling of melting gold inside your stomach after a long hug from a friend, or the rush of love when you see you mom for the first time in months.
- ◉ Being proud of myself.
- ◉ Passion.
- ◉ When you see yourself healing.
- ◉ Happiness.
- ◉ Love.
- ◉ Feeling confident.
- ◉ Being on the beach.
- ◉ Thankfulness toward myself.
- ◉ Happiness and pride in what my children have become.
- ◉ The feeling of dancing. It feels like you're inhaling your favorite things, like oxygen that tastes like calmness and creativity. It's so pure and just makes me dizzy with happiness.
- ◉ Confidence in myself, because if I wake up feeling confident, the rest of my day goes well.
- ◉ The feeling of the universe winking at you.

Now that you've read other people's favorite feelings in the world, think about some of your own!

- ♥
- ♥
- ♥
- ♥
- ♥
- ♥
- ♥
- ♥
- ♥
- ♥
- ♥
- ♥
- ♥
- ♥
- ♥
- ♥
- ♥

Now that you've reached the end, one thing I'd like you to take away from this is that you are absolutely not alone and you never will be. We are all surrounded by a community, including many people who can relate to your feelings and your journey. We understand that sometimes (or even a lot of the time) you can get emotionfull, and we understand that you may need help with that. If you can't find anyone to talk to, you can visit my website (positivepage.co). There, you can connect to people who have been through similar things and read some of the battles they've have had with their own mental health. We have to offer each other empathy and compassion to both heal the feeling of loneliness and clarify the miscommunication of mental health.

Something else I'd like you to take from this is that you are enough. All these feelings you have, the struggles you're going through—none of that will never change the fact that you are enough. Each and every one of your emotions is valid and deserves to be listened to. Never think that they make you less than or unworthy of love and support, because they don't. Your struggles don't make you unlovable. You are wanted, you are valid, and you are loved.

| | | | |
|---|---|---|---|
| Mind | mind.org.uk | The Hopeline | Call<br>1-800-273-8255 |
| YoungMinds | youngminds.org.uk | The Trevor Project | Call<br>1-866-488-7386 |
| Elefriends | elefriends.org.uk | American Foundation for Suicide Prevention | Call<br>800-273-8255 or text TALK to 741741 |
| Anxiety UK | anxietyuk.org.uk | Trans Lives | Call<br>877-330-6366 |
| BPD World | bpdworld.org | Papyrus HOPELINEUK | Call<br>0800 068 4141 |
| Anxieties | anxieties.com | SANEline | Call<br>0300 304 7000 |
| Rethink | rethink.org | Switchboard | Call<br>0300 330 0630 |
| National Alliance for Mental Illness | nami.org | Samaritans | Call<br>116 123 |
| United for Global Mental Health | unitedgmh.org | Shout Crisis Text Line | Text "SHOUT" to 85258 |
| SANE | sane.org.uk | Support Line | Call<br>01708 765200 |
| Mental Health America | mhanational.org | The Eating Disorders Association | Call<br>028 90 235959 |

● US Numbers    ● UK Numbers

# Acknowledgments

Firstly, I want to thank everyone who helped me with this book, either by writing your experience with your mental health, submitting a worry box, or even sharing with me your favorite feeling in the world!

Thank you to my friends for supporting me on the journey of writing and encouraging me to keep going even when I was doubting myself! Thank you for helping me with my mental health enough that I feel able to be open about my feelings in a real life book!

To my mum and dad, thank you for believing in me every day, for being proud parents and always wanting to share what I do with everyone you meet. Thank you for listening to me talk about things I am creating and supporting me with them in any way you can!

Thank you to everyone at Mango, specifically my editor, Natasha Vera, for giving me this opportunity and believing that what I have to say could help people.

Lastly, thank you to everyone who has supported my work, shared a post, commented with a message of support, and of course everyone who read this book! You've all helped me to find my voice and continue to share it which is such a lovely thing to give to someone.

Thank you and I hope this book helps you in return.

# About the Author

**Lauren** is an advocate for mental health who is learning about her own mind and just sharing her journey along the way. When she was a teenager she used her love for design to set up a website called The Positive Page to help people with self-care. The website and its pairing Instagram account grew as she started to raise awareness for mental health and openly discuss her ongoing struggle with Obsessive Compulsive Disorder and Health Anxiety. She wrote *Emotionfull* to provide a way to reach out to people dealing with similar struggles with their mental health, and to help them in the times they experience overwhelming feelings.

You can see more of her work by visiting www.positivepage.co. or following her on Instagram at @positivepage.co.

Mango Publishing, established in 2014, publishes an eclectic list of books by diverse authors—both new and established voices—on topics ranging from business, personal growth, women's empowerment, LGBTQ studies, health, and spirituality to history, popular culture, time management, decluttering, lifestyle, mental wellness, aging, and sustainable living. We were recently named 2019 and 2020's #1 fastest growing independent publisher by *Publishers Weekly*. Our success is driven by our main goal, which is to publish high quality books that will entertain readers as well as make a positive difference in their lives.

Our readers are our most important resource; we value your input, suggestions, and ideas. We'd love to hear from you—after all, we are publishing books for you!

**Please stay in touch with us and follow us at:**

**Facebook: Mango Publishing**

Twitter: @MangoPublishing

Instagram: @MangoPublishing

**LinkedIn: Mango Publishing**

**Pinterest: Mango Publishing**

Sign up for our newsletter at www.mangopublishinggroup.com and receive a free book!

Join us on Mango's journey to reinvent publishing, one book at a time.